THE ACCOMPLICES:
A Writ Large Press Book

theaccomplices.org

THE **ACCOMPLICES**

LETTERS TO MY CITY

Poetry & Essays

by Mike Sonksen

"To love L.A. is to love more than a city. It's to love a language. To do lunch or done deals or do the do and there ain't much in the way of duende. It's to love accents that change as swiftly as the street lights in this third world gangbang. One must understand that one speaks in minutes, freeway exits, cross streets, landmarks, availability of parking and the desirability of zip codes and prefixes."

–Wanda Coleman

I am still alive in Los Angeles!

I am still alive in Los Angeles
                    even as the price of rent rises
and gridlock strangles central arteries I'm old enough
            to remember
disco parties and the build up to the 1984 Olympics
and news reporters like Jerry Dunphy and Hal Fishman;
I remember when Fernando Valenzuela was a rookie
Years before I loved Wanda Coleman and Bukowski,
my first LA poets were Chick Hearn & Vin Scully
            —Then I read Mike Davis and Carey McWilliams
            and watched the gospel of Huell Howser
looking at things that aren't here anymore recalling former glory
like Ralph Story I'm still exploring
                    from Panorama City to Pomona

I am still alive
                    in Los Angeles as they build high speed trains
down Crenshaw and out into the San Gabriel Valley
changes in transportation for the new generation foreshadow
the nation's transformation as millennials on bicycles call
for the return of the Garden City; green in the 21st Century
is a matter of survival -- witness the revival of the wetlands
the riparian watershed is a sentinel for sustainability
unbridled consumption is a liability, observe residents
of Angel City playing their part restoring nature's heart

I am still
            alive in Los Angeles from festivals to funerals,
baby showers to weddings, each generation
                                    ever more beautiful

reality is ever musical—
throngs of people mix and match creating
the patchwork mosaic of multicultural souls coming
together to call LA home. The community is a poem
in progress called Los Angeles.The angels in a city singing
synchronicity from Central to Century City—
Olympic was 10th street and Pio Pico was the last governor
of California when it belonged to Mexico, he was born
a Spanish citizen— see the city Zen soaring to satori
on a Saturday morning circling the Evergreen Cemetery
or hiking up hills in Culver City

I am
still alive in Los Angeles as mamas monitor laundromats
from Lankershim to Long Beach, I walk the long streets
from Magnolia to Manchester, Rosemead to Redondo Beach
I am still alive in Los Angeles though there's no more open space;
most of the wetlands have been replaced by condos, Trader Joe's
and makeshift dog parks. The expanding corporate heart charts
a frenzied facelift of never-ending Christmas but only a few are
on that wish list. There's a generation of kids on snapchat
and commuters want that fast track
Alive in Los Angeles!

I am still alive in Los Angeles.
Thanks to family, friends and poetry. The past, present and future
of my city gives me energy. Untold generations of history from
Biddy Mason to Chavez Ravine to Toyo Miyatake punctuating
the power of place
turning the page sharing authority because we share
the story of the city unfolding—no hierarchy, we all belong
to this city—its oral *her-story*.

I am still alive in Los Angeles! Today I drive around
LA with my son and daughter like I once rode with my grandfather.

There's no more Perino's or the Brown Derby but there's still
Fosselmans, Cole's, Philippe's and the Pantry.
My children spill ice cream in the back seat,
Together we are alive in a city of destiny.
                              I am still alive in Los Angeles!

Community, Not A Commodity: The Ethics of Giving a City Tour

I have been curating city tours professionally since 1997. Over the last two decades, I have given thousands of city tours, most of them for Red Line Tours, the Museum of Neon Art and the Museum of Architecture and Design and more recently as an independent contractor. I am an advocate of community-based public history promoting the utility of historical knowledge to empower and deepen the public's connection to the past in a real-world platform beyond academia. A city tour is one of the most effective means to impart historical knowledge in an accessible and public fashion.

The starting point for giving city tours has been two-fold for me. As a third-generation Los Angeles native, my first exposure to history and geography were through listening to stories from my parents and grandparents. My grandfather schooled me on Southern California geography from a very early age. He told me many stories about the Great Depression, the streetcars of Los Angeles and how agricultural the region once was. We would drive in his car listening to jazz on 88.1 KKJZ back when the call letters were KLON. We drove everywhere from Long Beach to the South Bay to Downtown L.A. to the San Fernando Valley and the entire time he would tell me stories. At Point Fermin in San Pedro, he recalled proposing to my grandmother there in 1941. Almost everywhere we went he had a story whether it was the Griffith Observatory or the Central Library. I learned from him at a very early age the meaning and power of place and memory.

These family stories came to mean even more to me during my undergraduate years at UCLA shortly after the 1992 Rodney

King Uprisings as I took several classes on Los Angeles history, geography and urban studies. I read widely and books like *The Power of Place* by Dolores Hayden, *City of Quartz* by Mike Davis and writers like Wanda Coleman, Luis Rodriguez, Carey McWilliams and Lynell George further reinforced my interest in all things Los Angeles. My information sources for giving tours have always been a blend of both oral history from longtime residents and the many books I have studied on Southern California history, geography and architecture. My praxis is about uniting oral history with knowledge from books and more formal historical sources. The blending of these two together makes for a more balanced approach that unites theory and practice.

The Right to the City

I am aware how my neighborhood tours could be a gateway for boosterism, but my intent has never been to sell property or promote a neighborhood for redevelopment. Furthermore, cities across America continue to become more privatized, and this is problematic. In this era of gentrification and selling the city off to the highest bidder, this essay is also about the spirit of celebrating community. The French philosopher Henri Lefebvre coined the phrase, "the right to the city," and this is something I deeply believe. The city belongs to everyone. Lefebvre believed that public space should not be privatized. Lefebvre called the city "an oeuvre, that all citizens have a right to participate in." Urban historian David Harvey expanded on Lefebvre's philosophy, iterating further:

> "The right to the city is far more than the individual liberty to access urban resources: it is a right to change ourselves by changing the city. It is, moreover, a common rather than an individual right since this transformation inevitably depends upon the exercise of a collective power to reshape the processes of urbanization. The freedom to make and

remake our cities and ourselves is, I want to argue, one of the most precious yet most neglected of our human rights."

I have always felt that giving city tours celebrates this right to the city and that it reinforces the entire community and our common interests. This is why I like giving tours of neighborhoods beyond Hollywood and the more popular tourist pockets of Los Angeles. The entire city has the right to be celebrated. As the writer, professor and poet Dolores Hayden writes in her groundbreaking 1995 book, *The Power of Place*:

> "To look at ethnic and women's history as the missing mainstream experience means respecting the urban places that house ordinary working people. It means caring for the urban landscapes of South Central and East Los Angeles, Chinatown or Little Tokyo as part of understanding what it means to live in a city."

I have always taken the craft of giving a city tour very seriously. The research process is the most important element. Los Angeles Times reporter Steve Saldivar recently tweeted a statement by the UCLA Urban Planning Professor Dr. Eric Avila pertinent to this. Avila said at an event about gentrification that, "Activism that lacks knowledge isn't going to go very far." Deep knowledge of local history is equally necessary for giving a city tour or community activism. All the neighborhoods where I give tours of are areas that I know intimately from my experiential time spent there. The experiences range from having a previous job in the area to a family member or friend of mine that lived there. These experiences make the tour more authentic and ensure that the information provided is grounded. This methodology keeps the tour authentic and grounded in values that are lived-in.

Giving a city tour is about spotlighting the community, specifically the people and elements of the landscape that create its spirit. It is not about marketing or packaging it as a commodity.

Like Dolores Hayden, I am a practitioner of community-based public history.

What follows is a short list of core concepts I adhere to whenever delivering a city tour.

1. Get the History Right

The veracity of a city tour always begins with specific and accurate historical knowledge. A professional tour guide needs to be meticulous and get the history correct. It is important to name the names: the early architects, city founders, community leaders, the people who were instrumental in the formation of the specific neighborhood or location. Name as many of these names as you can and connect them to what they did.

We live in an era where history is often forgotten because time is moving faster than ever. The essayist Gerda Lerner explains in her book, *Why History Matters*, "Present-mindedness, a shallow attention to meaning, and contempt for the value of precise definition and critical reasoning are characteristic attitudes produced by mass-media culture. All of them run counter to the mindset of the historian and to the values and perspective historical studies provide." In addition to the short attention span of this time, and what Lerner states here, there are also many important historical figures that are overlooked in the coverage of history.

The forgotten pioneers are often women or people of color who played a critical role in the area's history. My sources for these names include not only books and documentaries, but from conversations with longtime community residents. The stories and folklore are priceless, and I do my best to collect these in the preparation of a tour. As much as I have studied Los Angeles and been all over the city, I always defer to longtime community members, and have them share their stories on the tour whenever possible.

Much of my approach in sharing public history has been influenced by the previously mentioned Dolores Hayden and *The Power of Place*. Her work advocates for a people's history. As she writes: "Public interpretation of historic places requires a broad understanding of urban history... Its best measure is shared meanings, Native American, African American, Latino, Asian American, and Anglo-American meanings, female as well as male values, children's experiences as well as grown-up patterns of life. It is city dwellers' shared lifetimes that create an American sense of place. In scale and approach, this is the opposite of top-down thinking that underlies urban design as grand-scale redevelopment planning practiced by American cities."

Hayden is critical of the top-down approach as this approach has minimal understanding of an area's history because it is much more focused on development and economics. She sarcastically calls this perspective, "the John Wayne view." Furthermore, she writes that it is usually marked in public as a sculpture of an old white man on a horse. In opposition to this, Hayden is interested in the people's history because it is the lifeblood of the city. Furthermore, she writes, "Listening to the resonant stories of working people in inner-city neighborhoods is the first step. Connecting the stories to reclaim the landscape as people's history is the next." The celebration of people's history triggers "social memory," and remaps the urban landscape. Finally, Hayden writes, "It is the controversial history Americans need to reclaim as our own, in order to give meaning to the contradictory urban landscapes of cities today, where wealth and neglect, success and frustration, often appear side by side."

One more element of getting the history correct is paying tribute to the *legacy businesses*. Recently, I collaborated with Traci Kato-Kiriyama, Kristin Fukushima, Allison De La Cruz and Scott Oshima for a series of walking tours of Little Tokyo. Traci, Kristin, Allison and Scott are deeply engaged in the Little Tokyo community and have been for many years. They each spoke about the few remaining legacy businesses in Little Tokyo. One of them is Fugetsu-Do Confectionary, a family run-bakery on First Street that has been open since 1903. It is the longest-running business in Little Tokyo and one of the oldest continuing businesses in Los Angeles.

Fugetsu-Do has faced some challenges in recent years and still manage to keep going. Traci encouraged the members of the tour to support Fugetsu-Do by patronizing their bakery in the future. During other tours, I have given in areas like Leimert Park, I have proposed similar requests to support the independent bookstore EsoWon Books and other legacy businesses I have encountered there like the World Stage. This idea of supporting longtime family-run businesses within a community also connects to the next idea which is sharing authority.

2. Sharing Authority

Another key concept from Hayden's work is the idea of sharing authority. Hayden references this concept from the work of the Professor and Urban Historian Michael Frisch. Frisch's important research offers great insight on the craft and meaning of oral and public history. His book, *A Shared Authority* emphasizes "oral history's capacity to generate alternative visions of American history and culture and to serve as a source of change, especially from the perspectives of minorities and women." Furthermore, Frisch writes that "what is most compelling about oral and public history is a capacity to redefine and redistribute authority, so that this might be shared more broadly in historical research and communication rather than continuing to serve as an instrument of power and hierarchy."

The concept of sharing authority translates into several actions within a tour. It means having long-term members of the community speak. When I have given walking tours of Leimert Park, I always bring the group to Ben Caldwell, the owner and founder of KAOS Network. Ben has been in Leimert over 35 years, and he has been involved on the ground level on many important projects in the area. Caldwell has always graciously received my tour groups whether it was students from Woodbury, LMU, University of Redlands or the walkers I brought from the Museum of Architecture and Design.

I have also had the poet AK Toney join me on the tour and share his poems and experiences. Toney brought me into the Leimert Park poetry community over 15 years ago, and he has been sharing his work there for 25 years. I have also had my former students; the siblings Dante and Monique Mitchell share their poetry on my Leimert tour and several others across the city. The Mitchells grew up in Leimert and were in my class when I taught at nearby View Park High School in 2008-2009.

Similarly, when I have done tours in Boyle Heights, I had lifelong East Los Angeles resident Tomas Benitez share his experiences. Benitez always dazzled the audience with his 60 plus years of stories. I also always have the Boyle Heights native poet Francisco Escamilla, aka the Busstop Prophet share his stories and poetry on the tour as well. In Boyle Heights we have also stopped at the Otomisan Restaurant that has been in the area 60 years along with the Rissho Kosei-Kai Buddhist Temple on East First Street.

I have featured other longtime community residents on other tours as well such as native Angelena poets and educators Rocio Carlos and Traci Kato-Kiriyama. As stated earlier, I always defer to longtime residents because their experience and knowledge trumps book knowledge or academia. This idea of sharing authority is common in all fields, whether it be in art museums or even medical research. The voice of community members is paramount in the historical process. Much of the backlash against gentrifiers and oblivious newcomers to an area is that they do not value the neighborhood history and the residents that have always been there. Newcomers may paint over a longtime sign or be unaware of the traditions that define the neighborhood. I have a deep respect for the longtime residents, their culture and their willingness to share their stories with me. This reverence is critical for giving a city tour or accurate historical account.

3. Debunking Stereotypes

On many occasions I have had travelers ignorantly ask me to take them to South Central, Compton or East LA. The tone in their question comes across in such a way that the area is dilapidated and dangerous and that they want to see the landscape they have heard about in a gangsta hip hop song or in a movie like *Colors* or *Boulevard Nights*. I always respond that these neighborhoods are beautiful places with humble working-class people and quite different than the stereotype they associate it with from a gangsta rap song or some exaggerated film. These misconceptions are part of why I began giving tours of areas like Leimert Park to show that these stereotypes are false.

At the same time, I am always cautious to let voyeurs know that I am celebrating the community in the interest of respecting the culture. It is not about marketing the real estate as a commodity. Respect and appreciation are always the underlying value that guides my explorations of the city.

A Final Word: Impact vs. Intention

Another element of debunking stereotypes is unraveling history beyond the most obvious known elements of the local history. Beyond the obvious implications about gentrification, some have been critical of city tours because they feel that the celebration of a specific community will inevitably lead to the exploitation and colonization of this area. There has been a historical precedent for this, and one example of the problematic relationship between impact and intention is the case of writer Helen Hunt Jackson and her book *Ramona*.

Published in 1884, many historians credit Helen Hunt Jackson's *Ramona* for romanticizing Southern California and inspiring thousands of East Coast Americans to move to California after reading the novel during the Boom of the 1880s. Phoebe S. Kropp reveals in her book *California Vieja* that this impact was the exact opposite of what Jackson intended. Jackson was attempting social commentary. "Woven in with Jackson's tale of romance was reproach for Californians' behavior and attitude toward Indian people," writes Kropp. A few years before Kropp wrote *Ramona*, she wrote the nonfiction book, *A Century of Dishonor*, which was much less popular. This earlier book was "a nonfictional account of the abysmal record of the United States' relations with American Indians past and present." Jackson diligently recorded the dozens of treaties and broken agreements that the American government reneged on with indigenous peoples from the 17th to the late 19th Century. Not surprisingly, this book was not very popular.

"When sales were slow," Kropp reports, "she (Jackson) sent a copy to every member of Congress at personal expense. While the volume caused nary in a ripple in the Capitol, she accepted a government offer to prepare a report on the condition of the California Mission Indians." Jackson was escorted around Southern California by real-estate promoter Abbot Kinney. After visiting Indian villages, crumbling missions and a few of the still-working ranchos, "she found material that she would later exploit for the romantic backdrop and charming characters she needed to tempt readers into her remonstration." Once Jackson filed her official report, she "decided to present her protests directly to the public in novel form. In a tale more personal than *A Century of Dishonor*, she hoped to 'set forth some Indian experiences in a way to move people's hearts.'"

Jackson said on many occasions that "she hoped *Ramona* would be the *Uncle Tom's Cabin* of Indian reform."

Not only was this intention not realized, but Jackson died ten months after *Ramona* was published. She did not live to see the book's impact. As Kropp reveals, Jackson's "audience was primed to respond to the romantic angle more than the social critique." *Ramona* became a runaway bestseller, and dozens of clever entrepreneurs around California capitalized on the book's popularity by staging Ramona pageants, building hotels named after it and even creating small souvenirs based on it. There is a city named Ramona in San Diego County, and part of Alhambra and Monterey Park was once called Ramona Acres at the end of the 19th Century. Moreover, there are still dozens of streets named Ramona in Southern California that were a direct response to the book's popularity. Jackson's intention of advocating the Indian's cause was not successful.

It is examples like what happened from *Ramona* that make long-term residents of certain neighborhoods wary of city tours and efforts to celebrate local history. Nonetheless, I believe that if historians and tour guides mindfully share their work responsibly and adhere to ethics like community-based public history and sharing authority, specific neighborhoods can retain their authentic charm and not be colonized or changed from their original spirit.

The bigger problem obviously is the power of market forces and how development always rules, but if policymakers can become even more conscious of promoting community-based public history, this could lead to more effective preservation of neighborhoods for longtime residents. As Dolores Hayden writes in her conclusion of *The Power of Place*: "Any historic place, once protected and interpreted, potentially has the power to serve as a lookout for future generations who are trying to plan for the future, having come to terms with the past." This is the spirit with which I give my city tours and write my essays and poems with. As Lefebvre said, everyone, "has a right to the city." Therefore, through the process of sharing authority, naming the names, debunking the stereotypes and promoting a community-based public history, we can come to terms with our past and map a much more equitable future.

Huell Howser and the
Gospel of Beauty

....

"California history and poetry, nobody cares about that." I knew in my heart he was wrong but there wasn't much I could say at the time. "It might be romantic, but if you want to write and make a living, write for an advertising agency or write a screenplay. Not California history and definitely not poetry, do you want to starve?" My dad would laugh and tell me not to be sophomoric. I was 21 years old in my third year at UCLA and on this particular night I was riding in the car with my father to visit my grandmother at her house in Inglewood. Before we arrived, we argued some more about my interest in poetry and career choice as a writer. My studies at UCLA brought into focus my own third-generation Angelino status and after studying with Mike Davis and Urban Planning professor Brian Taylor, I had made up mind despite practicality or whatever jokes my dad had.

"My son, the poet," he would say with a smirk. We would visit my grandmother and eat dinner with her. KCET was almost always on in her home; I remember that my grandfather always watched the *Macneil/Lehrer News Hour* and after he passed in 1985 my grandmother continued to. They were old school LA in every sense of the word; I remember they subscribed to the *Herald-Examiner* rather than the *Los Angeles Times*. We watched Huell Howser together with my dad and her many times over the years. Back in the mid 90's, Huell Howser was about the only thing my dad and I could agree on.

The truth is we'd visited many of those places over the years but my dad took it for granted because he was born in Los Angeles in 1941 and seen it all before. He'd lived through the history I was studying about and didn't think it was as significant as I did. My dad had taught me about the architecture of Frank Lloyd Wright from an early age and I had a natural interest in maps and geography by kindergarten that was fostered by lots of drives with my dad and both of my grandfathers.

My dad and grandmother liked Huell because it triggered the nostalgia of their own childhood and experiences growing up in Southern California while it was still being built. For me, "California Gold" reinforced my own burgeoning interest in this history; I saw Huell as a messenger to stick to my own California dream.

My first few years at UCLA I discovered that looming behind my interest in Los Angeles geography and history was a massive treasure trove of books, film and music. Huell affirmed this interest every time I saw his show. I watched it even more the older I got. Shortly after I graduated from UCLA I emailed him a few of my poems of L.A., but I never heard back from him. Though I had hoped he would respond, looking back I don't mind that he never replied, because just seeing his joyful spirit on television over all these years made me happy and reminded me to keep taking drives and study the landscape. Huell helped me see that my dad and grandparents were an amazing source and I started taking more drives with my dad and asking my grandmother even more questions.

Huell helped me realize I had family roots on both sides that traced back to all four of my grandparents growing up in Los Angeles during the Roaring 20s.

Before she died in 2003, my grandmother told me many of her memories of early Los Angeles. Places visited by Huell would trigger conversation points and memories every time we'd watch it. She knew Southern California well because she was born in 1917 in Highland Park in a homestead near Avenue 59 and York Blvd. She attended Polytechnic High School when it was located on the present site of Trade Tech College. She lived the last 52 years of her life in Inglewood. Her husband and my grandfather, George Sonksen attended Manual Arts High School and was a carpenter/contractor that built many homes around the San Fernando Valley and in Inglewood along Crenshaw in the 1950s. He also worked a few years for McDonnell Douglas during the Second World War. The more I uncovered my own family history the deeper I got into my studies. Huell's portraits of people and their stories helped me realize how meaningful every story is.

My dad was born in Los Angeles around 87th and Central and they moved to Inglewood when he was 10. He attended Washington High School a few years behind Surf Rock legend Dick Dale, known for his band the Delltones and later rediscovered thanks to *Pulp Fiction*. My dad loved Huell's portraits of out of the way entrepreneurs like Fosselman's Ice Cream in Alhambra or the famous donut man in Glendora. Like many other families, lengthy drive missions across Southern California were regular weekend activities for my father and I during the 1980s.

It's easy to see how Huell provided the common ground for people to relate and meet on like he did for my dad, grandmother and me. We had many joyful moments watching Huell Howser. As the years went on and I gradually began to get published, my dad gradually warmed up to my interest in California history— maybe not poetry, but that's another matter. Either way, Huell Howser's show was an important bridge.

Reflecting on Huell's passing I am reminded of the early 20th Century poet Vachel Lindsay. Lindsey espoused a philosophy he called "The Gospel of Beauty." Lindsey walked across America between 1908 and 1914 performing poetry and sharing the gospel of beauty wherever he could. He was called "the Prairie Troubadour." Part of the gospel of beauty, Lindsay declares is, "the new localism: the things most worthwhile are one's own hearth and neighborhood. We should make our own home and neighborhood the most democratic, the most beautiful and the holiest in the world." Lindsay was known for an enthusiasm perhaps unmatched until the rise of Huell Howser.

Huell Howser embodied Vachel Lindsay's wandering spirit of making every site and moment holy. Huell was a California Troubadour and wherever he found himself he was celebrating the beauty of that moment whether it was the Point Fermin Lighthouse, the Apple Pan or some small local eatery he stopped by. "Wow! That's amazing!" Huell's gospel of beauty was an ability to shine a bright light on everything he saw and touched. Huell didn't push some predetermined agenda like some reporters or journalists; he just encouraged his subjects to tell their own story and allowed them to shine in their own natural light.

In this age of critics, pundits and know-it-alls Huell ebulliently showcased real people and cataloged the heartbeat of California winning fans from all walks of life. Ironically, Huell worked for "Entertainment Tonight" in the early 1980s before he started with KCET in 1985; this makes sense in retrospect because his "California Gold" segments and his other KCET shows are light years away from the artifice of Hollywood glamour and tabloid television. After beginning his Los Angeles days in the belly of the artificial beast, Huell ran in the other direction and found California Gold in the everyday landscape, reminding us to behold the beautiful in our own backyard. DJ Waldie wrote in the Zocalo Public Square, "Howser wasn't just pitching the muchness of California, an abundance anyone should be able to see unaided. He was pitching the almost infinite otherness within the ordinary of California, particularly when California is considered with joy."

Considering California with joy could be as simple as appreciating those days when it's clear enough to see snow-capped Mt. Baldy. Huell helped a generation of Californians realize the majesty all around us. There's no question that Huell's influence on the growth of the study of California History is every bit or more influential over the last generation as the work of writers like Mike Davis and Kevin Starr. "California Gold" has been seen by millions over the last 25 years, there's an archive of 2000 episodes. In 2011 Huell donated all the tapes to Chapman University to be digitized as well as gifting the school 1800 books on California history for their library.

My dad always saw Huell Howser as a modern-day Zen-master. Huell's love for California transcended party divisions, his enthusiasm for people and places was a powerful touchstone that brought our family together and I'm sure countless others like mine. Like Vachel Lindsay, Huell Howser was an emissary for the gospel of beauty. So long Huell, thank you for reminding Californians to celebrate the gold in our own backyard: You are one of the brightest stars that ever beamed in the firmament of LA Letters.

Iconic Vision: The Architecture of John Parkinson

....

Iconic Vision: John Parkinson, Architect of Los Angeles is Angel City Press's book on the storied life and career of John Parkinson, architect of LA City Hall, the Memorial Coliseum, Bullocks Wilshire and Union Station along with over 400 buildings throughout Southern California, Seattle, Salt Lake City, Dallas and more. Despite all that he accomplished, this book is Parkinson's first biography. This essay takes a long look at Parkinson's vast body of work as it is outlined in the book.

Parkinson was a contemporary of Frank Lloyd Wright, Richard Neutra, Rudolph Schindler, Le Corbusier, Paul Williams and other celebrated early 20th Century architects, but his name is much less known and surprisingly little has been written about his extensive design oeuvre from 1890 to 1935. Author Stephen Gee's narrative tells background stories behind his important projects like the Memorial Coliseum and City Hall and traces the trajectory of Parkinson's life from his childhood in England, his adventurous escape west that included Seattle first before arriving almost penniless in Los Angeles and then Parkinson's long reign as dean of Los Angeles architects.

Gee's detailed volume effectively argues that though the architectural giants named above are more internationally famous than Parkinson, none of them have produced as many long-lasting icons as Parkinson did. The author makes a strong case for Parkinson noting again and again that many of the projects built by Parkinson are still standing after close to a century.

Only fifty Parkinson buildings remain in Downtown. Spring

Street being the Old Bank District has almost a dozen Parkinson structures between City Hall and 9th, including the building the Last Bookstore is in. I've noted in a previous column that there is a plaque honoring Parkinson on the building near the northwest corner of Spring and 5th. Walking past the Parkinson plaque on a Thursday in August 2013 I couldn't help noticing a large potted tree blocked the plaque's visibility. Though I'm sure this act was unintentional by building management, it is an appropriate metaphor.

Parkinson's work is everywhere in this city, but many have never seen him. If I hadn't known the plaque was there from my past knowledge I would have missed it entirely. Parkinson's work like the plaque has been there all along whether anyone notices. Gee's book portrays Parkinson as a humble man that was more concerned with producing structures that will stand the test of time than fame. On this standard alone, it is safe to say Parkinson achieved this goal and then some whether or not the average Angeleno knows his name.

Spring Street is the obvious place to begin. In 1903 Parkinson designed the Braly Block at 4th and Spring, the first skyscraper ever built in Los Angeles. It put Parkinson on the map in the city and sooner than later his practice began to flourish. By 1904 Parkinson moved his own firm into the building and he was barraged with requests for his services. The prosperity of the era fostered Parkinson's use of experimental new architectural techniques. Project after project, from the Alexandria Hotel, Rosslyn Hotel, to being commissioned by USC, structures in Pasadena, Bullocks Wilshire, Parkinson worked on many of the region's biggest structures from the turn of the Century till his death during the Depression. Parkinson died while Union Station was being finalized and it's appropriate that his last project was an icon analogous to City Hall, the Coliseum or Bullocks Wilshire. His body of work displays a wide range of versatile styles over the years from Beaux Arts to Art Deco.

The new Spring Street Park is surrounded by three different Parkinson Buildings, including the Braly Block, the Rowan Building and the Title Insurance Building across the street. The Title Insurance Building was once known as the "Queen of Spring" and this is where Parkinson's practice was while he designed City Hall in the mid-1920s. Gee describes further, "the exterior terra cotta displayed a travertine-like finish, complemented inside by real travertine and marble in the public areas. Artist Herman Sachs was recruited to decorate the lobby ceiling and Hugo Ballin to create the murals above the street entrance." Resembling a deco cruise ship, the Title Insurance Building like so many Parkinson structures still looks monumental.

Another important Parkinson design is the Alexandria Hotel on Spring and 5th. Though it may be taken for granted now, when the Alexandria was built in 1906 it was the finest hotel in the city. For the first two decades, U.S. presidents, royalty and movie stars stayed there. Gee writes, "the main restaurant, finished in fumed oak and Italian marble, had thirty-foot ceilings and elaborate glass chandeliers. The second-floor banquet hall, decorated in ivory and gold, contained private rooms where business leaders could meet behind closed doors." The Banks-Huntley Building, a block south of the Alexandria is an art deco gem in mint condition. Adjacent to the Spring Street Bar, its smooth design falls in line with all his other work on Spring.

Completed in 1923, Parkinson's Memorial Coliseum is the only stadium ever used in two Olympic ceremonies, 1932 and 1984. It's fair to say that the Coliseum was the first of his major iconic works. Gee reveals how Parkinson's love for his city guided his practice with projects like the Coliseum. "He viewed the ambitious undertaking as his civic responsibility and agreed his firm would work at cost while he donated his own services." USC immediately began playing football in the stadium. Later the Dodgers would play four seasons there, the Los Angeles Rams and later the Raiders played NFL games and presidential campaigns, concerts and religious leaders appeared at the coliseum.

Around the same time as he designed the coliseum, Parkinson designed USC's Administration Building in an Italian Romanesque style. The success of the structure led Parkinson to work on twenty projects for USC though several never materialized. Nonetheless eight of Parkinson's USC buildings remain in use to this day.

The sheer number of Parkinson buildings still standing is astounding. Besides his collection on Spring Street, there are two classic Parkinson buildings on Hollywood Blvd.; there's Fairfax High School, Manual Arts High School, the Homer Laughlin Building where the Grand Central Market is, Santa Monica's City Hall, and the list goes on and on. Gee comments on Parkinson's legacy: "Bullock's Wilshire remains one of the most masterfully crafted structures ever conceived in the city and is enjoyed every day by the students and faculty at Southwestern Law School. The administration building at USC is still the most recognizable structure ate the university. And nearly seventy-five years after the first train arrived, bustling Union Station remains one of the city's most beloved architectural icons."

Considering Parkinson's tremendous architectural legacy, *Iconic Vision* is an excellent name for this book. Furthermore, the subtitle, "John Parkinson architect of Los Angeles" is also fitting. The iconic power of his work makes this label accurate because Parkinson's track record speaks volumes. Gee's book puts Parkinson's work in its appropriate historical context. Curious urbanists and architectural students will find an encyclopedic account of the great architect's busy life. The mix of historical anecdotes and vintage documents and images presented also show how prolific the man was. Salute to his storied legacy and his extensive body of work, John Parkinson will always be one of the most iconic architects in the landscape of LA Letters.

Marguerite Navarrete:
A Teacher Ahead of Her Time

Some people are so influential and instrumental in our development that we do not even recognize their magnitude until they are gone. I first realized this when my grandfather died in 2002. A huge core of my value system, attitudes about life, and personality came from him. This piece is not about my grandfather though, this essay is a tribute to my 3rd and 4th grade teacher, Marguerite Felice Navarrete.

The seeds she planted in me over 30 years ago continue to sprout and there are not enough kind words to express how exemplary her teaching skills were and my deep gratitude to her. Ms. Navarrete, as we called her, was an award-winning teacher and highly skilled in her vocation. She worked at three schools in the ABC Unified School District in Cerritos and Hawaiian Gardens from 1974 until her retirement in 2010. I was enrolled in her class for two years in a row at Patricia Nixon Elementary, which was the first of three schools she taught at. I was blessed enough to have her two years consecutively with a cohort of students that all stayed together because she had been so successful with our class. In my third-grade year, it was a combination class of grades two and three. In the following year, it was a combination of grades three and four.

The UCLA Writing Project

The summer before I entered Ms. Navarrete's class she was one of the Fellows in the distinguished "UCLA Writing Project." Founded in 1977, this annual 4-week program instructs teachers in several techniques on how to teach all aspects of writing. Each year hundreds of teachers from all academic levels apply for the program and only a select few are chosen. One of their core concepts is that teachers must learn to be great writers themselves to teach the craft. It is a testament to her veracity as a teacher that she was selected to participate in this program. As one of her students, I can testify that she effectively shared with us all her knowledge about writing and self-expression.

I entered Ms. Navarrete's class in the 3rd grade in the fall of 1982, just a few months after her time in this program. She was a charismatic teacher that inspired us every single day. I remember her mentioning UCLA and how she had studied there, but obviously at 8 years old I had no idea about how influential and groundbreaking the program that she was enrolled in was. After I got my Masters' degree about 30 years later, I learned about the UCLA Writing Project and its storied history.

I remember doing a lot of writing in the two years I studied with Ms. Navarrete. We kept journals religiously, wrote many short essays, brainstormed, created clusters and did free writes. She taught us a strategy called, "the Power Paragraph." She also taught us reading strategies and applied them in class when we read Shakespeare. We read *Romeo and Juliet*, *Julius Caesar* and *A Comedy of Errors*. She taught us how to read these texts by breaking each section up into small chunks and we would read it as a class. She made sure we understood everything. There were some that thought she was crazy to teach Shakespeare to 3rd and 4th graders, but she knew exactly what she was doing.

Her teaching skills were so incredible that our class was on television. We were featured in a segment on a local ABC show called, "Eye on LA." The word had quickly spread around our school, the district and Southern California about what Ms. Navarrete was doing with our class. I still remember the day when the camera crew came to our classroom. They filmed her teaching and interviewed many of the students. I watched the segment when it aired back in 1984, but I do not have a copy of it. Perhaps one day I can come across the footage, but for now the memory is firmly embedded in my mind.

Years later when I was in graduate school at Cal State L.A. in Dr. Christopher Harris's class, "English 504," I studied writing theorists like Mike Rose, Peter Elbow and Don Murray. I learned about how in the 1970s, these thinkers and several other writing theorists revolutionized teaching writing. I also learned that UCLA and their Writing Project program had been one of the epicenters of this because of professors there like Mike Rose. After learning about Peter Elbow's ideas on free writing, I realized that I had already been exposed to these exact concepts from Ms. Navarrete in the 3rd and 4th grade. She figured out how to take these ideas and work them into our curriculum. There was a collective consciousness around America of progressive writing teachers during this time and she was at the forefront applying these ideas with us.

The Spirit of Los Angeles

I was in her class from the fall of 1982 to the spring of 1984. The spirit of the Los Angeles Olympics was in the air. We would often talk about Southern California and current events. I even remember her showing us a short documentary about "Being Chicano." Our class was very multicultural and she epitomized the optimistic spirit of not only the 1984 L.A. Olympics, but the collective consciousness that Southern California was becoming during the era of Mayor Tom Bradley. Her persona epitomized the spirit of Los Angeles and multiculturalism.

One of the highlights of my second year with her as a 4th grader was a class field trip we all took to UCLA. My mom took the day off from her own teaching job in Long Beach and came with our class. We toured the campus and had a magical day there. That was the day I decided I wanted to attend UCLA and sure enough, 8 years later I did.

In the fall of 1992, I entered UCLA as a freshman. This was the first big dream of mine that came true. Furthermore, this was also the period in my life where I decided I wanted to become a writer. I began writing poems about the city, neighborhoods and the social issues following the 1992 Rodney King Rebellion. Though I had written poems way back in Ms. Navarrete's class and had enjoyed writing essays and poems in high school, it was really my freshmen year at UCLA where I took the initiative and started writing earnestly. It all unfolded very quickly and before I knew it, I was filling up multiple notebooks with poems, essays and various rants. The concepts she had planted in my consciousness early, manifested in a big way during this time. I had excellent English teachers in high school and I even kept in touch with a few of them in the following years; nonetheless I never kept in touch with Ms. Navarrete after I graduated from elementary school in 1986. It was not that I did not want to keep in touch with her, it was just that at such a young age, I was not as conscious of staying close with former teachers. Nonetheless, I have thought about her many times over the years and even looked her up on the internet in 2010, but I never did contact her.

A Trailblazer Ahead of Her Time

In early June 2016, a friend of mine from my elementary school days that I have not seen in 15 years sent me a text message saying that Ms. Navarrete had just died. She was only 66 years old. I never did get a chance to thank her for all her help and inspiration. She planted the seeds in me so early that I did not even realize that I owe so much of my writing and teaching career to her. The values and techniques she taught me were so deeply embedded that they were second nature. I had been practicing them and living them for so long that perhaps they were even taken for granted.

As I mentioned above, after studying some of the history of Writing Theory in English 504 in 2013, I began to realize just how groundbreaking Ms. Navarrete was. I knew way back when I was in her class that she was great, but now I realize how she was among an elite group of trailblazing educators pushing forward new ideas about writing. Moreover, she was doing this with us in the 3rd and 4th grade. She made writing fun.

Years later when I had moved away from home for the first time and was attending UCLA, I remembered all the early writing techniques she taught me and I began to write compulsively. By the time I was 23 in 1997, I was a published poet and my work was being read across the Los Angeles basin. Around this same time, I started freelancing as a journalist and by my mid-20s, being a writer was a central layer of my identity.

Flash forward to June 2016, I heard about her passing just in time to attend Ms. Navarrete's funeral. It was held at Rose Hills Memorial Park and I saw several teachers from my elementary school there. I had been out of touch with all of them since at least 1986, but ended up speaking to my first-grade teacher for close to an hour at the reception afterward. There was even a brief open mic at her service and I said a few impromptu words. I was looking for other students that had been in my class with her, but I did not see any. There were other former students, but it seemed as if they were from her later years.

I came to find out from what everyone said that she was a private person. I affirmed this further when I was unable to find much about her personal information online. One of the only stories I could find on her was connected to the UCLA Writing Project and it was an article from when she was there in 1982. I found out that she was born in December 1949 and that she graduated from Lynwood High School in 1968. She started teaching at Nixon Elementary in 1974 and was there until 1987 when she went to teach at Carmenita Middle School. I graduated from Nixon in 1986 and never spoke to her again, though I had thought about her hundreds of times, especially after I really embraced writing in the 1990s. I always meant to get in touch with her.

Goodbye to a Steel Butterfly

Following Carmenita, she went to Fedde Middle School in Hawaiian Gardens in the late 1990s and taught there as well. She retired in 2010 and eventually passed away on May 30, 2016. One of Ms. Navarrete's longtime colleagues from her days at Carmenita, RoseEllen Shea extolled Ms. Navarrete in an online post:

> "She was large in the lives of many, loud in her quiet, child-like in her wonder, a believer in magic beans, a steel butterfly, a storyteller unparalleled, a lioness for kids, a kind tinker for those who live in the land of misfits and broken toys, a firecracker, a belly laugher, and I got to be her friend."

Like the sentiments expressed above by RoseEllen Shea, I am grateful that I got to be her student. There are not enough words available to ever properly pay tribute to her. I will always regret that I never did have a chance to speak to her again or thank her for all she did for me, but I will continue to pay it forward. I am now not only a poet and journalist, but I have been teaching English for over a decade. I hope to be half the teacher Ms. Navarrete was.

Sometimes

....

A Golden Shovel for F. Douglas Brown & Mike Davis

The warm winds blow sometimes
making me feel like I
am one with the city. I feel
connected to the landscape like
the Santa Monica Mountains are my
spinal cord—my backbone that only
can be seen from an airplane. I see my friend
in every intersection—my destiny is
to uncover the stories—to incite others to the
other side of reality—the beauty in the city

The beauty in the city is what I
sing—I see the spectrum where I live
from a Garden City to dry canyons in
the foothills above the flatlands where the
Postmodern populace reinvents the city
tropicalizing cold urban space to make a place of
                        refuge for a city of angels

THE 562

The 562 is a nexus: A suburban, urban cross-section.
A small town, big city, affluent, yet gritty,
The 562 is somewhere between Hollywood and Irvine,
Santa Monica and Anaheim.
The 562 is a good time because its people are down to Earth.
Blessed by birth to be born where the vibes are warm,
catch that cool ocean breeze blowing in from the beach.
The clouds come from the south as the coast winds
around the peninsula of Palos Verdes.
The temperature is perfect.

    This land was once marshlands
                    and Willow thickets,
    intercepted by the L.A River.
    Now surfers & grandparents kick it.
    The 562 is all-American multicultural,
    folks from Iowa to Cambodia,
    El Salvador to Ethiopia,
    aviation Okies and the aerospace industry.
    Denizens of Long Beach groove
    to Snoop Dogg & Sublime,
    garage rock and freestyle rhyme.
    On the streets of Long Beach
    you can find oil in Signal Hill,
    Broadway's alternative lifestyles—
    art in the East Village,
    Downtown lofts and Rockabilly chillers!
    And how many Poly players are in the NFL?!

        From Joe Jost's to the Prospector, Cohiba
        to The Blue Cafe, drinking Sangria on a hot day, barflies

cruise from the 49er to Belmont Shore, Fern's to the
V-Room. The 562 is a window into
the future with lots of history. Like the powerful
earthquake of '33, the Pike is the place to be,
and let's salute Cameron Diaz and her flavorful family.
Respect to Lakewood, Cerritos, Bellflower, Paramount,
Downey, Hawaiian Gardens, Whittier, Norwalk, Cudahy,
South Gate, Compton to damn near Bell Gardens.

> Not to be confused
> with the 310,
> this is the 562!

In the middle of So. Cal, but its own little world,
It's another beautiful day at El Dorado Park,
in the place of my birth and the home of my heart

This is the 562.

Driving Down the 105

On many late nights, I've had to drive home on the 105 freeway. In 1997, a few weeks after I graduated from UCLA, I was hanging with old friends in Cerritos on a July Saturday night. I left at 1AM to get back to my old apartment in Culver City. I had KCRW on and they were playing a mix of electronic music.

I got on the 605 north from South Street and after a few exits I took the 105 West. The 105 is the newest freeway in LA and it was finally finished in the mid-1990s. Some of the excitement also came from the high-speed train in the middle of it. The Green Line Metro train runs in the middle of the 105. Back in the 1990s, this was very exciting for all of us that grew up in Southern California with no high-speed trains or even the Pacific Electric streetcar from the days of yore. The electrical wires over the train tracks made the night lights over the freeway and cityscape look technological and futuristic. We used to say *Blade Runner.*

On this evening, driving home on the 105 with electronic music playing was surreal science fiction. Twinkling lights on the Rancho Palos Verdes peninsula glimmered off in the distance. Downtown LA's small cluster of skyscrapers held court a dozen miles north. Miles and miles of small houses framed by rows of palm trees stretched in every direction. Warm air blew into my car through the open window. I decided to open all the windows and turn the music up. I felt the wind blow through my hair and I smelled the summer night.

The landscape coalesced with the music. This was a few years before I had a cell phone so I was truly one with the moment. The radio played, "Inner city life, inner city pressure."

When I looked at my speedometer I noticed I was driving around 85. Next thing I know an Acura blasts past me in the left lane. He must have been moving well over 100 miles per hour if not faster. A few seconds later in the far-right lane a souped-up Honda Accord speeds by even faster. Right after that another sports car I barely see comes up right behind me, in my lane, forcing me to accelerate.

I put my foot on the gas and hope that he will change lanes. The music continues to play. Next thing I know, I see I'm going over 100 miles per hour!

Zooming past the Central Avenue exit, I switch lanes. The guy behind me keeps going and I was thankful he did. Just when I was about to catch my breath, a few seconds later, one more speed demon zips by swiftly on the left. I'd never seen so many wild drivers together at the same time. I thought I was in *Mad Max*.

I slowed down and turned the music off. I was glad the road warriors were gone. The explosive mix of reckless driving, late vibes and music made it more surreal than a cyberpunk novel or video game. Like *The Fast & the Furious*, these racers were heavy on the pedal. I got on the 405 north, got back to my apartment and was thankful to be home.

I can still see them zooming past me like Vin Diesel or Mel Gibson. It was one of those nights where the truth is stranger than fiction.

Long Beach's Cambodiatown

In late 2011, the 20-block stretch of Anaheim Street from Atlantic to Junipero in Long Beach was officially declared "Cambodia Town." A large blue sign commemorates this on the district's borders. While the LBC's neighbor to the north, L.A., has districts like Thai Town, Little Armenia, Little Ethiopia,

Koreatown, Little Tokyo and many more, the equally diverse Long Beach is known for Bixby Knolls, the Pike and Belmont Shore. Once known as "Iowa By-The Sea," the Cambodia Town designation is truly historic: it's the first ethnic district in Long Beach to be officially recognized by the city.

For stakeholders in the Long Beach Cambodian community, this is epic. Dating back to a cadre of Cambodian students that attended Long Beach State over three decades ago, the Long Beach Cambodian community has grown to almost 70,000, the largest concentration of Cambodians anywhere outside of Cambodia. They are especially thrilled to call Long Beach home, since they were forced out of Cambodia under murderous conditions.

Though I was born in Long Beach, most of what I know about Cambodia Town I learned from Prach Ly. Prach came to Long Beach from Cambodia at age 5 and has been here ever since. In 1999, just out of Jordan High School, Prach recorded a bilingual hip-hop album that described the horrors of Cambodia's Killing Fields. Prach had listened to his elder's stories and retold them in a hip hop vocabulary. Furthermore, he blended English with his native tongue, creating a tour-de-force unlike any other Long Beach hip-hop artist. Somehow the album was bootlegged and taken to Cambodia, where it went viral.

With his music Prach was telling stories that had only been whispered. His public breakdown of Cambodian history was groundbreaking on many levels. Soon Prach was revered in his homeland and in demand around America, on both the university lecture circuit and underground hip-hop scene. I met Prach in 2003. On three separate occasions, he has given me personal tours around Long Beach. On each of these missions he drove me down Anaheim Street.

The Cambodian community in Long Beach is centered on Anaheim Street, with another Cambodian enclave in North Long Beach. The stretch of Anaheim Street is certainly the symbolic home. One of the first places Prach drives me to is the United Cambodian Community (U.C.C.) office at Anaheim and Dawson. We walk upstairs and he introduces me to Chad Sammeth, the Project Coordinator and Community Organizer at U.C.C. He conducts workshops on "Financial Literacy," as well as always being available for any questions anyone in the Cambodian community may have. He has helped many Cambodian immigrants read contracts, open a bank account, read the fine print on financial forms, and so on. I saw several Cambodian grandmothers thank him wholeheartedly on their way out the door.

The U.C.C. was recently funded by the California Endowment, and Chad is one of three full time employees. "The other two happen to be my personal heroes and mentors: Sara Pol-Lim (Executive Director) and Raymond Chavarria (Project Director). I love what I do. I am surrounded by people who are driven by passion and purpose," he says. He explains his motivation, "One of my major sources of inspiration comes from our elders—Killing Field Survivors. During the Khmer Rouge regime in the early '70s, they were forced to leave all things familiar to escape death. Families were separated and scattered around the globe. In the past 30 years they struggled with language barriers, cultural barriers, social and economic barriers, emotional and mental trauma. I would be lying if I said that I understand what they went through.

"The atrocities they experienced are beyond my comprehension. To a large extent, our elders are still a maimed and fragmented generation," says Sammeth. "To say the least, they've been through a lot and they are tired. They just want to hold on to what little joy they have left. We as children often forget that our parents are people too. They have done their part in giving their children a second chance at life. Now it's up to us, the next generation, to become their success stories."

Prach and Chad are walking the walk. Prach travels the college circuit performing his hip hop and lecturing on Cambodian history, while Chad stays home in Long Beach handling the day-to-day operations at the U.C.C. "Prach and I met at a community function several years ago. It didn't take long for us to become close friends, because we are both doers. We are kindred souls working towards a common goal to serve a healing community. We make a good team," said Chad, describing their partnership.

Cambodia Town is lucky to have these two young lions working so hard. The district's future is promising, but the built environment along Anaheim Street in its current state— mostly low-slung older buildings housing several Cambodian restaurants nestled between carnicerias, used car lots, laundry mats, Pho spots, and Smog Check Centers—could use some attention. The decaying streetscape is waiting for new life.

The U.C.C. office has a large window looking southwest onto Long Beach's skyline. Chad looks out the window often, imagining Cambodia Town's future. He would like more pedestrian life, outdoor restaurants, a small park, and even some public art. He has a vision to merge architecture, sustainability and urban design. He sees Cambodia Town as a destination district, much like Retro Row on 4th Street or Belmont Shore, serving as a cultural and financial hub in the middle of Long Beach.

An avid surfer and a magnanimous man to all people, Chad is as committed to his community as he is to the waves. He loves Long Beach's diversity. He wants new people to know about Cambodia Town. He conducts monthly walking tours, inviting guests to "come taste the flavors of Cambodia." Along the way he shows a mural of a traditional Cambodian Buddhist

Temple and explains that the Mark Twain Branch of the Long Beach Public Library has the largest collection of Cambodian books in America.

"I have a message to my peer groups," Sammeth says. "Ages 40 and under: We have little to no excuses not to succeed. We now live in the information age, an era of self-made teenage millionaires. Lacking a college degree or conventional education is no longer a valid excuse. If you can't find a job, create one. Technology has leveled the playing field of opportunities. The only barriers and boundaries that exist, are the ones that we allow to exist. We are just as capable as those who are making headlines because we have access to resources too. Our people have had a rough history. We cannot change the past, but we can change how we feel about it, learn from it and move forward. Let's move forward... together!

"Get off the sidelines and onto the field. We need more teammates. If you don't understand something, ask. If you don't agree with something, suggest. If you criticize, be constructive, not destructive. Eliminate the doubts and suspicions that grind down at our progress. Rumors and gossip to a community is like cancer to a body. Instead, let's nourish the hearts and minds of our generation with encouragement and optimism. It's been over 30 plus years since we arrived in America, we've come a long way from refugees. We've made strides in recent years. It's time we make leaps and bounds."

After hanging with Chad, Prach Ly and I ate at a Cambodian Restaurant called "Sophy's" on Pacific Coast Highway, just north of Anaheim Street. In just under three hours Prach treated me to a great meal, he showed me his family's Buddhist Temple, the mural by the library and most importantly introduced me to his comrade Chad Sammeth. Together they look at Long Beach's skyline and imagine the future.

On Location: North Long Beach

Long Beach is like its northern neighbor Los Angeles with its many eclectic and diverse districts. In the past, I have written about Cambodia Town in Long Beach, Bixby Knolls and the historic architecture of Downtown Long Beach. This essay focuses on an underappreciated but equally fascinating section of the city: North Long Beach.

Oklahoma to Samoa

North Long Beach is one of the most diverse neighborhoods in Southern California and has sizeable populations of African-Americans, Samoans, Cambodians, and Latinos and in the past, was known for residents from Arkansas and Oklahoma. The area is amid an upswing and many more new developments are on the way as we speak.

North Long Beach is north of Bixby Knolls and south of Compton and Paramount. The district's eastern border is Lakewood and on the northeastern edge it's Bellflower. There are many in Downtown Long Beach that try to lump Bixby Knolls into North Long Beach but they are two separate districts. North Long Beach really begins north of Del Amo and it is much more working class than Bixby Knolls. The 91 freeway is on the northern edge, but there's a small slice of North Long Beach that is north of the 91 before it becomes Compton. On the western edge is the 710 and Los Angeles River, but there is also a small triangle-shaped portion of North Long Beach that is west of the freeway and river. The two biggest streets in the area are Atlantic and Long Beach Boulevard, but other significant thoroughfares include Cherry, Artesia Boulevard, Del Amo and South Street.

Like so much of Southern California, the roots of North Long Beach are agricultural. The landscape began in the early 20th Century as open pastures of asparagus, sugar beets and dairy farms. For much of the 20th Century the residents were truck drivers, shipyard employees and factory workers. The current population is just under 95,000. According to census figures from 2010 about 54% are Hispanic, 21% are Black, 11% are Asian and about 8.7% are non-Hispanic white. There is also a sizable Samoan and Tongan population.

A Suburban-Urban Cross Section

My mom taught elementary school in North Long Beach at Jane Addams for 15 years from the mid-1970s until 1990. She told me that when she started there, the school was widely known across Long Beach for being the most diverse elementary in the district. The neighborhood itself is a patchwork landscape that is urban and suburban simultaneously. Well-kept houses exist on quiet tree-lined streets and a block over there may be small apartments, pawn shops and liquor stores.

Over the years I have driven through North Long Beach countless times and have had many friends that have lived and worked in different corners of the district. Marcella Carlson, born in 1938 lived most of her early life in North Long Beach. "I was born in Long Beach, California, at the Bixby Knolls Maternity Hospital," she says. "My first memory of North Long Beach was living in Carmelitos Housing Project. We lived near some of my mother's family. I was in Kindergarten, at Jane Addams Elementary." The Carmelitos Housing Project is still in North Long Beach just west of Orange Avenue and in between Del Amo and Market Avenue. Carmelitos was built at the end of the Great Depression just before the start of World War Two. The project has undergone many ups and downs over the years, but it is currently in better shape than ever and now known for a large community garden just east of Atlantic.

Marcella Carlson remembers the days in her early childhood when much of North Long Beach was open space and the landscape was not as packed with houses. Her father was in the military and after the war finished, they bought a home in North Long Beach at 65th Street and Cherry Avenue, about two miles north of Carmelitos. She went to McKinley elementary school and remembers riding the bus to get there. Her dad was an iron worker and her mom worked at her grandmother's Mexican restaurant. One of her strongest memories from her childhood was the heavy fog that blanketed North Long Beach during the cold months every year. "One year it was so thick," she recalls that her dad "walked in front of the car to find our way home. Today, I rarely see fog."

During the 1950s and into the 60s, the district's population continued to increase and both the 710 and 91 freeways were built through the area. More homes were built and many apartment buildings also emerged. The population for many years had been working class whites and many from Midwestern states like Arkansas and Oklahoma. As surrounding areas like Compton became more African-American in the 1970s, North Long Beach did gradually as well. Reverend Leon Wood has been a minister at two different churches in North Long Beach over the last few decades. He tells me that the neighborhood is now, "in transition." Wood wants more collective action and he does his best to connect all the different groups. He says that the Samoan and Tongan population are his "forgotten people." He says this because though they have a significant presence in the area they are not as politically visible as the Latino, African-American or Cambodian populations. He has a few Tongan Godchildren that he does his best to look after and help. Wood and his wife run a nonprofit organization called "Success in Challenges."

A Voice for the Voiceless

Wood works with all segments of the district. On the day I met with him, he had just finished meeting with a local gang leader.

Simultaneously Wood also works closely with city officials and prominent businessmen. He tells me he is not interested in judging people, he's too busy making a difference and he does his best to advocate for those that don't have a voice. He hopes that community members in North Long Beach and across the city can become a "united team for progress." He also hopes for a "renewal of caring." He cares deeply for the young people of North Long Beach, telling me incredulously that, "some of the youngsters of North Long Beach have never even seen the water five miles south down Atlantic." At the same time, as much as he has compassion for the youth, he does his best to instill their entrepreneurial spirit. "We're not in the position for leisure," he says, "It's time for hard work."

Wood is keenly aware of historical trends and tells me that, "gang activity follows the employment cycle. When industry moves out, gangs move in." For this reason and more, his nonprofit offers employment referral services, job placement assistance, tutoring, and personal, career and family counseling. Over the years Wood's programs have been sponsored by organizations like the Long Beach Transit, St. Mary's Hospital and the Port of Long Beach among many others. Over the course of the afternoon I spent with him, I saw him greeted warmly by dozens of diverse residents.

The educator and poet Sarah Tatro grew up in North Long Beach. She moved there in October of 1986 after moving numerous times and attending 8 different elementary schools. She recently told me, "After living as transients for several years, North Long Beach was a middle-class haven in my 12-year-old eyes. To say the least, it was the first place I lived long enough to feel like home." She attended Lindberg Junior High and then Jordan High School. Her family lived on Osgood Street, a half a block from Deforest Park, which runs along the LA River bed. She spent a lot of my time riding her bike and walking her dog in the park or up on the riverbed. The neighborhood provided enough safety for her to begin writing, but "it was also full of streets you didn't walk down, day motels, drug dens, crying babies in front yards, gang affiliations, kids trying to posture themselves against threats. We all survived in our own ways. I tried a few crowds: skateboarders, cheerleaders, drama kids, beach bums, death-rockers, and even the Christian rockers."

Tatro tells me that the longer she lived there, the more aware she became of the social class levels of the surrounding neighborhoods. "Lakewood was a couple miles east and was just one class above ours," she remembers. "Bixby Knolls was a couple miles south and was full of older, more affluent families. Compton, to the north and west of us, already had a reputation for being ruled by gangs. North Long Beach was somewhere in the middle of it all a mix of grit and family homes."

The neighborhood was a big influence on her and she was discovering music by groups like The Cure, The Smiths, and New Order. She wandered around the park with her dog and tried to write song lyric in her head. "Since I have zero musical training or talent," Tatro acknowledges, "these lyrics became poems. I wrote about other people's drug use or suicide attempts. I wrote about my own invisibility and longing for love." Her youth in North Long Beach led to her becoming a writer filled with empathy. "I'm not afraid to speak painful truths. When people share their darkest corners, I don't flinch. It's all beautiful, the grit and softness of life," she says.

North Cambodia-Town

Though the Anaheim Street corridor three plus miles south of North Long Beach is known as Cambodia Town, there is a significant number of Cambodians living in North Long Beach and there has been since the 1980s. Prach Ly, the well-known Cambodian activist and hip-hop artist spent most of his childhood in North Long Beach. His family lived in an apartment at 69th Street and Long Beach Boulevard from the time he was about 7 to 17. The building is two blocks south of the Compton-Long Beach border. Ly attended Jordan High School and credits his love of hip-hop to growing up surrounded by it. Ly recently drove me around his old stomping grounds and pointed out apartment buildings where Cambodians lived. The one he grew up in was a building with a Cambodian manager and this helped to encourage his parents to move there.

Ly reminisced while we drove down Long Beach Boulevard, "Before the iPad and xBox we played outside a lot. Hide-n-seek, cop-n-robbers, kick the can, marbles, throwing coins. We even played tackle football on cemented concrete." Growing up in North Long Beach during the late 1980s and early 1990s was at times intense for Ly. "I've been jumped, stabbed, shot at, caught in a middle of a drive by, it got to the point where I was immune to the violence," he recalls.

Despite all the trauma he faced and all he went through, Ly remains upbeat and optimistic. "A lot of things have changed in North Long Beach, not just in North Long Beach but throughout Long Beach, and it's for the better. It's cleaner and safer. I'd like to personally thank the city officials and acknowledge the police department in doing so. And the people and citizens of Long Beach for making the change within themselves by helping to be the change. Change start from within," Ly says. Ly prides himself on his ability to reach out to others and to be positive in the face of negativity.

In 2013, Ly co-founded the Cambodia Town Film Festival with his friend the filmmaker Caylee So. So lives in North Long Beach with her husband and a few years ago the film she made for her Masters' Thesis at Chapman College won the top prize. Ly and So hope to highlight Cambodian cinema because Cambodian arts, music and film were nearly destroyed during the Killing Fields. "A quarter of our population was either murdered or starved to death," Ly says. "The Khmer Rouge regime was on a mission to turn back time, no social class and declared their takeover as 'Year Zero.'" Ly takes his role very seriously as an artist and activist. He's glad that he can make a difference. "We are the children of the 'Killing Fields' and Long Beach being the largest population of Cambodians outside of Southeast Asia," Ly notes, "we feel like we have a responsibility to make a change."

Caylee So is encouraged by seeing Cambodian-American youth in North Long Beach, "embracing their dual cultural identities." One of the biggest intentions of their film festival is to, "Increase the visibility of the Cambodian community, especially through the arts." The Cambodia Town Film Festival is an annual event every September.

Prach Ly also introduced me to Suely Saro. Saro is a Cambodian-American woman who works as a field representative for Senator Ricardo Lara of the 33rd District. Saro says, "The increasing number of Cambodians moving to North Long Beach creates a relationship with Cambodia Town. Cambodians influence neighbors and friends in North Long Beach to shop, eat, and hangout in Cambodia Town and vice-versa." She told me that on April 17, 2015, the Cambodian Genocide Remembrance Day was conducted in Uptown Long Beach.

On the corner of Atlantic and Artesia Boulevard is Jordan High School. In years past the school had a bad reputation but there's been big improvements over the last several years. Tiffaney Mocsary Gardea has taught at Jordan for 12 years. For the last five years she has been the lead teacher for their "Excellence Through the Arts," program. Gardea told me that when she first started they had a huge turnover in principals, with almost one per year, but then they switched the school over to a credit recovery campus and "We increased our graduation by about 100 students." She remembers, "One student told a heart wrenching story at graduation about being 'just another statistic on the streets' until she realized with the credit recovery campus she actually had a chance. She did it, she pulled through and was the first in her family to graduation."

Gardea has been teaming up with other teachers to create authentic real-world experiences for their students. They have worked with representatives from the Toy Industry for a toy design project that the students really love. "One of our graduating seniors may even be to make his toy design a reality and our business advisory board can help make that happen," she says. "I love going to work in North Long Beach where I know I can really make a difference. We are all trying to make a difference for the better at Jordan."

Uptown Long Beach

Another group in North Long Beach doing their part to improve the area is the Uptown Business District. Located on Atlantic near 56th Street, the group works with local stakeholders, clergy and community organizations. I briefly met with the Executive Director Sean Duren. They are working with Rex Richardson, the Long Beach 9th District Councilmember on the "North Long Beach Whole Village Initiative." This program aims to improve outcomes and conditions for boys and young men of color. The program includes after-school workshops, mentoring, college readiness and opportunities for jobs and internships.

On the corner of 58th and Atlantic is the Michelle Obama Public Library. The 25,000-square foot facility is state of the art and a focal point for the community. There is also a new fire station coming and the Deforest Wetlands Restoration which will convert 34 acres of overgrown vegetation into land for public use. The wetlands will be for both wildlife habitat and hiking in the area just east of the Los Angeles River, north of South Street.

In 2009, a local group of educators and writers published an anthology of nonfiction essays, poetry, oral history and fiction about North Long Beach. Edited by Rachel Potucek, the collection includes over 50 writers and over 30 plus paintings and photographs accompanying the text. The book is bursting with community pride. A short essay celebrates the multicultural mix of kids at the skate park at Houghton Park, just south of Jordan High School. Another piece laments the loss of the movie palaces in the area and one memorializes the long-gone Dooley's Hardware Store that was on Long Beach Boulevard for so many years. Moreover, the collection highlights little known facts like how Long Beach Boulevard was one called American Avenue and that North Long Beach was once called Virginia City in its earliest days. The book's proceeds were all donated to the Fairfield YMCA, serving youth in families in the North Long Beach community.

Recently Def Jam Recordings signed the young rapper Vince Staples, who grew up in North Long Beach, near Ramona Park. Staples has a song called, "Norf, Norf," about growing up in the area. Though Snoop Dogg grew up in Long Beach, he is from the Central District and went to Poly High School, significantly south of North Long Beach. Staples is one of the hottest young rappers in the game these days and he proudly claims North Long Beach. His debut album was released last month.

North Long Beach is not often mentioned when one thinks of the greater Long Beach area, but the district is a soulful, diverse area with a bright future. There is a large group of committed citizens doing their part to improve their district. Salute to North Long Beach for being a dynamic neighborhood in the geography of L.A. Letters.

Los Angeles A to Z

Around Arcadia, Alhambra and Artesia after Atwater and Arleta along Atlantic, big rig trucks blow by Balboa, Bellflower, Beverly Hills & Burbank but not Bergamot. Burbs be calm connectors cool out in Carson, Crenshaw, Covina, Cudahy, Culver City, Coldwater Canyon & Commerce Casino. Commuters catch the crunch down Doheny delivering dudes to Downey, don't dismiss Dolby in Downtown Disney, eventually east of El Monte is easier in El Segundo, exit Etiwanda

for Ford factories far faster than Flower or Figueroa, Fontana flora & fauna, Groves got ghost in Glendale on GlenOaks, gates closed in Garden Grove, Gardena & Garvanza. How many hosts had high hopes in Hollywood? How about Halloween's home in Hawthorne? Who got hoodooed on Hoover? How about hype in Hacienda Heights? Is it intricate on Imperial? Is industry invisible to individuals in Inglewood? Is it indivisible to jump junctions on Jefferson? Juxtapose jets again, justice is jettisoned in a jurisdiction kicking it in Koreatown, catch karma clowns cataloging key kinetic characters living in Los Angeles & Lennox, look at Long Beach's long streets like Lakewood

learn about La Mirada, La Palma, La Puente, Lomita & Lawndale meet Morrissey in Montebello, Monty in Montrose, make a mark in Monterey Park, maybe more in Monrovia. Nobody knows Norton on Normandie or north of Northridge, nor their neighbors on Nordoff in North Hollywood O Olympic, Olive & Olvera Street, order over in Orange County, operate on Ontario's observatory   Pedestrians pose in Pico Rivera, pursuing passion in Pasadena, pour it out in Paramount queue up quickly at Queen of the Valley, quest quintessentially for quality at quiet cannon

Remember Robertson, the Rose Bowl, Rosecrans, Rose Hills & Rosemead. Somewhere south of Santa Ana, Sam Sanders sings San Marino songs saluting Soto Tourists take trains to Trader Joe's, Tulare, Turnbull Canyon, Torrance, Tujunga & Tarzana

under Universal City up to Union Station up above University voyagers vibe on Vermont & Victory viewing Van Nuys, Valley Village & Victorville's vicinity wandering west to Watts, watching westerns on Winnetka, West Adams & Westchester examine Excelsior's exposition along Ximeno exiting Xanadu You got young yogurt on York Boulevard, youthful unity in Yosemite

Zankou is zen, zone into zeitgeist zip up your zoot suit & zoom zoom zoom Zion to Zuma!

I GREW UP IN LOS ANGELES

I grew up in Los Angeles during the time of the Riots,
a city of love, a city of violence.
Suburban homes are seldom quiet
overworked parents, teenagers defiant.
I grew up in Los Angeles where latch key kids
handled their business, look over your shoulder
& don't be a target,
a city of song, a city of sorrow
I grew up in Los Angeles watching Laker Championships
Magic Johnson, Shaq & Kobe Bryant
a city of love, a city of violence.
Magic visited patients at Daniel Freeman Hospital
one of them was my grandfather in 1984.
My grandparents grew up in Los Angeles
during the Depression & Zoot Suit Riots.
A city of compassion, a city of smashing.

I grew up in Los Angeles where sand drawn lines
defined the times of April 29th, 1992.
I grew up with a bridge-building crew aware of the chaos
but focused on the payoff
a city of fire, a city of desire
My parents grew up in Los Angeles in the Age of Elvis & Eisenhower,
Surf Safari, Endless Summer,
a city of memory, a city of mystery,
I grew up in Los Angeles with three generations of family
navigating the landscape to make way for me
I grew up in Los Angeles in the age of Reagan, Crack & Aids
a city of clubs, a city of drugs,
early adventures at UCLA began in 1992

out of the ashes of the uprising came the New,
a city of beauty, a city of duty.

I grew up in Los Angeles building unity through art, music & poetry
connecting communities with the word, a city of curves, a city of verbs,
I grew up in Los Angeles building bridges forming coalitions,
a city of visions, a city of decisions, a city of maps, a city of traps,
a city of machines, a city of dreams, a city of tracts, a city of facts,
a city of beaches, a city of teachers,
a city of Dodgers, a city of fathers,
a city of working mothers, a city of broke lovers,
I grew up in Los Angeles in the age of each other
a city to know, a city discovered
I grew up in Los Angeles during the time of the Riots,
a city of love, a city of violence.

Arrival Stories

....

If you listen they will tell you:
      I was born in Vancouver, which is a beautiful city
      We came from Paraguay, in South America.
      I was born in Seoul, Korea. We lived there until I was five.
We packed everything up into our Toyota Corolla.
      I drove cross-country and went across Oklahoma and Texas
      I really came to L.A. by way of Las Vegas.
I often think of L.A. as being like a big circus
      Man, I am constantly tripping on this city.
My grandparents helped build Little Italy
      their story is also tied up with Pasadena
          My father was this young kid from Oregon
          his first job was in a nursery.
          I loved instantly the casualness of outdoor living
          and passion for sports
          Back then, the barn had a creek running by it.
          They came in about 1911. He opened a barber
          shop on North Broadway, a couple of blocks
                south of New Chinatown.
      My mother would always tell me stories
      about Japanese occupation
Grandpa Duval worked as a car salesman
          My family is of Indian heritage.
          I went to East L.A. College and studied
          Spanish, French and English.
      My dad spent a lot of time at the YMCA.
          I studied Interdisciplinary Studies at Cal State LA.
      My parents were born in Kenya as was I.
          I worked in a laboratory at UCLA.
      They also lived in South L.A., at 89th and Vermont.

My mother was in a biker gang in Colorado.
        She came out from Kansas City for five dollars.
Los Angeles is a dream. The pace is slower
                24 blind teenagers
                from the Los Angeles Junior Blind League
                    taught me how to read the city
        You have the Transverse Ranges that end with
        San Gorgonio and go west all the way out to the ocean.
And the Peninsular Ranges end with San Jacinto
                    and go all the way down into Mexico.
        It was a night of instrumental hip-hop,
        and free hand drawing.
        But I usually just danced all night.
        in spite of having grown up in
        antagonistic political systems,
        we held a compatible sense of ethics,
        We took nineteen days crossing the Pacific.
            So why should we hold grudges?
            Our final port-of-call was San Francisco.
            There was a lot of optimism and hope.
It was the 'Age of Aquarius' around the world
        We took Eka Loa to see Totoro at the Egyptian
            I was born in San Fernando—the "San Fernando"
    in Trinidad not the Valley
            I mean, there we were in a tropical paradise—
our weekends were filled with trips to the beach
                there were Afghan refugees and live musicians.
        People would go across the canyons. Guys and girls.
            And there was a sense of community because
            you had long hair. Maybe you had a guitar
                Rabab, harmonia, tabla, Afghan ghazal singers,
one hundred cousins of every single religion & nationality
        When they spin they expel their ego
                and bring in the ecstasy of the source Creation.
            I would go to Barnsdall Park & sit

on the grassy hilltop
I'd have to make runs all over town
almost every day
—usually in various degrees of heavy traffic.
I mastered the art of not hitting the brakes
on the freeways of L.A.
I became a maestro of the slow crawl
I fell in love—I was wooed by the weather,
I walk in the canyons and climb the local hills,
I look out to the Channel Islands
and see a ship on the water
the common denominator is,   people come to L.A. to make
a life for themselves.   It's like being
on the yellow brick road,   it's wonderful
you can really leave the past behind   I made a determination to turn
the physics of hip-hop into a workbook
Memories become fables, families immortalized
& mythologized for their survival
Reborn upon   Arrival

A Field of Great Streets

1.

The dawn of a new Los Angeles begins with a field of great streets A built environment redefined to improve the quality of living An infrastructure of beautiful boulevards, arcaded walkways and public parks Citizens under the order of art, reveling in a framework of urban choreography A platform for the body public, the landscape as subject A culturally vibrant district, sustainable, green, walkable and connected

2.

A city of civic engagement begins with a field
of great streets promoting interaction in the civic axis, open
grid patterns, sidewalk activities, metropolitan movement
depends upon access the dialectic between the public
and pedestrian eschews the backward design of exclusion
vibrant urban action is magical urbanism

3.

Long before the super expressway
there was Sepulveda and Imperial Highway
Great streets are essential arteries,
the nucleus in the heart of the city

Districts like Thai Town and Little Armenia are touchstones for international citizens Koreatown, Little Ethiopia, Historic Filipinotown, Chinatown, Little Tokyo, Little Bangladesh, the backbone is local small business, the Central American Corridor, California San Salvador, specialty markets, family eateries, density entwines webs of parallel existence thick in the heart of the inner city

Families depend upon community safety, green belts and parks are the place to be social relationships define the city, power exchanges unfold geographically class divisions are divided by topography, the landscape reflects the sociology the only way to decipher the cartography is to spend time walking the city

4.
Figueroa is the intersection of the avenues,
Highland Park to Eagle Rock
Let the people walk from
the Southwest Museum to the Coliseum
One time for the Gold Line, take the Blue Line to LA Live

Lankershim Boulevard holds the North Hollywood Lit Crawl
The poetic free-for-all is a literary victory in the heart of the Valley

Sherman Way is where auto body and furniture shops melt with Thai restaurants, across from the car wash, Sherman runs below descending planes it's another hot day in the 818

Van Nuys Boulevard runs by a replica of LA City Hall, covered bus stops, Discount stores, banquet halls, shoe shops, the Van Nuys Bazaar, Dried palm fronds, Pupusa patios, country stores, rooftop billboards

Reseda Boulevard runs west of Cal State Northridge, Northridge was once called North Los Angeles, Reseda bridges Tarzana to Granada Hills to Ventura Boulevard, the Valley is a landscape of cowboys and aerospace

Ventura Boulevard is the Valley's Wilshire, Studio City to Calabasas, Sherman Oaks and Encino, Learning Centers, plant on premises, Audio specialists, Coldwater Canyon, delicatessens, private lessons

5.
Western Avenue extends from Los Feliz to Palos Verdes,
the peninsula to the Observatory, a Los Angeles story

from Koreatown to South LA, Western goes a long way

Westwood Boulevard bisects an urban village,
Bruin Walk to Wilshire, the Westside Pavilion,
stimulate student grammar with art at Armand Hammer

Crenshaw Boulevard starts at Wilshire and ends in the South Bay,
The heart of Black LA from Jefferson Park to Inglewood
Forever an iconic neighborhood

Central Avenue hold a legacy of sound, the Dunbar crown
connected At 43rd, the Lincoln Theater and now Three Worlds
Café Central gave birth to jazz in LA

Pico Boulevard is an avenue of stars, Santa Monica to Staples Center,
Mid-City through Pico-Union, Rimpau, Roscoe's and Robertson
Pico lives Los Angeles lessons

Venice Boulevard runs from the Boardwalk to the Fashion District,
Downtown to Dogtown, Mid-City to Mar Vista,
Sepulveda to La Cienega, Centinela to La Brea

Hollywood Boulevard was once called Prospect Avenue
A dirt road with strawberry fields and pepper trees
Now counterfeit celebrities parade Grauman's Chinese

Cesar Chavez was once Brooklyn Avenue and it's still Sunset
The sun has never set on Boyle Heights, the history
Remains ripe in this mecca of LA life

Gaffey in San Pedro slides just west of cargo cranes
The old hillside of gun batteries is now Angels Gate
The Korean Friendship Bell dwells by Croatian Place

6.
        The Missing Persons sang "Nobody Walks in LA,"
        in the days of Reagan, it used to be that way

A generation later it's a brand-new day
The bike coalition choreographs passageways
Los Angeles walks the four corners of the city
Decode the districts, grapple with the grid
Hack the cardinal directions, investigate the intersections
The goal is to make it safe for all, a city more
equitable and accessible

7.
Multicultural communities for mobility,
the pedestrian bill of rights on people street,
connect the dots, create vibrant public space, embrace
multimodal transit, pay homage to local place-making, support
existing businesses, calm the traffic, increase the walking factor,
engage the youth as community ambassadors
Make it Mar Vista, Revisit Reseda, rethink street theater,
Reimagine Cesar Chavez, reconfigure the infrastructure,
these upgrades can be made without displacement, all residents
deserve safety, in a generation of gentrification, it's time
for consideration and respect to those who came before
working together as a city we can do more;
the dawn of a new Los Angeles begins
with a field of great streets
a built environment redefined
to improve the quality of living.

It's No Place for Kids

....

Skid Row intersects with the Toy District
but don't get it twisted it's no place for kids.

Skid Row shrinks and grows when the sun sets.
The industrial back streets of Skid Row by day
do brisk business. Hong Kong Wholesale,
Apparel, Textile Warehouses, underground sweatshops,
fabric stores and Fish Markets. When commerce closes
down go the metal garage doors and then come the homeless.

By day they can be found in single-room occupancies,
basketball courts, porta-potties, brick buildings, back alleys.
The Midnight Mission and League of Women
are a small safety net. Still not nearly enough beds,
cardboard boxes are used instead; spread over 10 square
blocks. Lighters flicker on and off, some are here on
purpose, some on accident and some were left.
All of them are sleeping with one eye open, trash cans on
fire, packs of tents, the brave ones sleep alone.

It's a short distance between Heaven and hell along the Nickel.
Los Angeles Street is the Berlin Wall—a liminal thoroughfare
east of Luxury Loft Land. Steps away from Adaptive Reuse,
a few blocks away from Pussy & Pooch. Ice Skating in Pershing
Square, the Oscars at the Biltmore, Hybrid Showroom-Boutiques
in the Historic Core are next door to Skid Row watering holes.
This has happened before: The Lower Eastside and
San Francisco's Mission District. Redevelopment/Gentrification.
How do we reconcile these merging worlds?

If we had the answers, would Skid Row still be here?
Would they sleep somewhere else? Would they sleep
in the River? To those stressed about the homeless,
what do you suggest? People aren't garbage, they can't be
swept in the recycling bin. The homeless were here before
the lofts, they were here before the Art Walk. They are
a product of Trickle Down Economics, a product
of the free market. Emerson spoke of the Over-Soul,
today's man is much more cold, we live in the richest
country in the world, but you'd never know on Skid Row.

> Skid Row intersects with the Toy District
> but don't get it twisted it's no place for kids.

The Riots Were the
Week Before My Prom

The riots were the week before my prom
a month & a half before graduation
Southern California was a time bomb

race relations warring like Vietnam
my crew more like the United Nations
the Riots were the week before my prom

So Cal needed mindfulness like Thich Nhat Hanh
Multicultural coalitions for communication
Southern California was a time bomb

Tired citizens needed a new song
All the broadcasts played nonstop frustration
The Riots were the week before my prom

Three months later I moved out of my Mom's
UCLA my emancipation
Southern California was a time bomb

Poetry & music made it more calm
Journal writing became my salvation
The Riots were the week before my prom
Southern California was a time bomb

ODE TO THE
LOS ANGELES RIVER

I sing of a River dammed, dumped, pumped and diverted;
I sing of a River they almost murdered.
I sing of a River the people forgot,
I sing of a River that flows from the rocks…

I sing of a River rushing from Mountain slopes,
snowmelt below Mt. Wilson, the mouth of the Arroyo.
I sing of a River where the shifting bottom of soft
sedimentary sandstones and clay mixes with gravel
washed from seasonal runoff.

    I sing of a River less celebrated than world waters,
      still powerful enough to wash away a village.
      I sing of a River that switched beds,
        underground moisture in the watershed.

I sing of a River where much of the water never reached the
sea – forming marshes, lagoons and mud flats.

    I sing of a River with a huge underground reservoir
      beneath the San Fernando Valley,
        I sing of the River that built this city.
        I sing of a River that provided life
          for the Tongva Tribe. Later to be called
            Gabrielinos, they lived amidst the willows,
            edible berries and sycamore trees.
            I sing of a River where steelhead
            were hunted by grizzlies.

I sing of a River with an archipelago of birds, insects and
tiny green particles, foam bubbles, towering power lines,

cottonwood trees, tadpoles and morning frogs. I sing of a River
where pelican's songs echo off canyon walls.

>I sing of a River unknown to many,
>perhaps first seen in *Grease* or *The Terminator*,
>I sing of a River that's always been here.

>I sing of a River with tributaries, like the Rio Hondo.
>I sing of a River with a confluence in the Arroyo Seco.

>I sing of a river weaving through crossroads
>of freight rails and intersecting freeways.
>I sing of a river below Metrolink and Gold Line trains.

I sing of a River with a bevy of bridges.
>Merrill Butler built iconic bridges
>>in the City Beautiful tradition.

I sing of a River where 44 pobladores
established the pueblo of Los Angeles in 1781
at the Confluence in the name of Spain and King Carlos the Third.

I sing of a river that was here long before sig alerts.
I sing of a river before concrete, squatter camps
>and floating cans of beer.
I sing of a River paved in concrete by the Army Corp of Engineers.
I sing of a River resurrected one pocket park at a time.
>Blades of grass breaking concrete,
>>riparian wetlands in the Compton Creek,
>>Oleanders in Atwater, re-instate the native garden!

Lewis MacAdams founded the Friends of the Los Angeles River
with the power of the word. Like John Kinsella says,
>>"Poems can stop bulldozers."

>I sing of a River where wetlands
>and washes once dominated
>witness the return of the watershed.

LA AUTHORS

Is it the sunshine or catastrophes?
Flash floods or the traffic?
Something about Los Angeles
makes music, makes magic.
The muse of Los Angeles
makes artists get active.
Behold the lore of LA authors!
Behold!! Who's rocking' the populace
in the postmodern metropolis?
LA Authors.

Starting with Charles Fletcher Lummis
Sunshine looms large in literary Los Angeles.
From the myth of Ramona, Pueblos,
Californio Ranchos,
Orange groves & the Arroyo Seco —
Expatriate artists of the 1890s
brought the first sunshine wave of LA Authors.
Boosters blew the trumpets on the Golden State's landscape,
sun for 300 days, a cure for old age,
find the fountain of youth in Los Angeles.

Hyped up pamphlets let the world know.
"Land of the sunshine,"
"the new Eden."
It was manifest destiny,
but it wasn't heaven for everybody.
Besides the boosters there were debunkers, socialists,
expatriate poets, leftist screenwriters. Fitzgerald,
Louis Adamic & Jake Zeitlin,

Nathaniel West was one of the best,
the City in Flames in the Day of the Locust.
The underground intelligentsia of artists & authors
living in Echo Park bungalows,
McCarthy called it red hill.
Sinclair yelled oil!
Behold the lore of LA Authors!

Chandler & Cain were kings of writing Noir
Detective novels in the lost streets of Bunker Hill
where Fante celebrates staircase fire escapes & lost love.
Long before Rodney King there was the Zoot Suit Riots,
the LAPD & Navy fools fought with Pachucos
in the Sleepy Lagoon
Carey McWilliams knew the deal:
Fire Factories in the Field...
Palm trees are swaying in the wind
as the sunset begins its Twilight on Franklin.
And What Makes Sammy Run?
Is it the architectural illusion?
Hollywood tycoons and the American dream
If he hollers let him go,
Get your Jazz on Central Avenue
Robinson Jeffers & Langston Hughes
Ray Bradbury wrote Martian Chronicles,
L. Ron Hubbard wrote science fiction into Scientology,
Charles Bukowski in single room occupancies wrote
sublime poetry about the plight of modern man
with a beer can in his hands.
Venice beats off Abbott Kinney and every time
I'm in Venice Jim Morrison speaks to me...
Behold the Lore of LA Authors!

Rocking like Rockabilly car clubs,
the Carpenters, Beach Boys.

Grease, disco & roller skating
Singer-songwriters in Laurel Canyon like
James Taylor & Joni Mitchell
sang the real deal in the Hollywood Hills
basking above Babylon & hedonism before
hippie folk maidens became pop rock musicians.
Rocking the Rainbow room like Led Zeppelin
selling platinum, radio free Hollywood
Hotel California, the Doobie Brothers
Play that funky music white boy
Behold the lore of LA Authors!

Brett Easton Ellis tells us about
gilded youth snorting white rails
in Beverly Hills, Less than Zero.
Walter Mosley with Easy Rawlins
The Devil in the Blue Dress & Little Richard.
Barry White grew up near Willowbrook
Motown came out west with the Jacksons
Lewis MacAdams dug Miles and the Birth of the Cool
James Ellroy kept LA Confidential, the Black Dahlia
To Gabriel Garcia Marquez' Magical realism.
Hunter S. Thompson's New Journalism,
South of No North in the City of Quartz,
Reeling in the years in the Ecology of Fear
Mike Davis & Magical Urbanism hit like
Joan Didion's White Album…
Thomas Pynchon to Luis Rodriguez,
Lynell George to Ruben Martinez
Wanda Coleman & Exene Cervenka.
check out the L.A. sound selectors.
Punk rock pop Underground poets
Urban planners Klein, Soja, Jello Biafra
Rollins, Ellyn Maybe, spoken word artists
Got trails blazing. Paul Vangelisti,

John Thomas, Lawrence Lipton & the Holy Barbarians,
Stuart Perkoff & words raisin' roofs like
A Mic & Dim Lights, Poetix, Beyond Baroque.
Ginsberg got naked folks.
Welcome to the West Coast's Poetry & Jazz Festival
The truth is stranger than fiction
its surreal living these conditions,
William Gibson Science Fiction.
Cyber punks on super expressways.
Ghetto bird copters every day.
Hollywood loves the apocalypse
The coast is toast!
Earthquakes, flash floods, El Nino
Armageddon, busted bridges
Waves are crashing on the edge of the continent.
Is it the city in flames or another day in paradise?
Sunshine or noir — Baywatch or Blade Runner?
Stay tuned for another long hot summer
Santa Ana warm winds keep blowing
Creative juices keep flowing &
the list of LA authors keeps growing!

LA Authors making Music loud like
Sunset Strip rock'n'roll soul
Doors, Van Halen, Motley Crue, Guns 'N'Roses
Ice Cube, NWA Dr. Dre, Pharcyde
Snoop Dogg, Freestyle Fellowship,
Hip-hop, metal, bedroom producers,
Turntablists & poets
Behold the lore of LA Authors!
Behold!

Mapping Chester Himes: Southern California and Social Realism

In the history of Literary Los Angeles, Raymond Chandler was perhaps the first author that skillfully mapped every corner of the city within his narrative framework. The seminal African-American author Chester Himes is another writer that mapped Los Angeles with the same veracity as Chandler. This edition of L.A. Letters looks at two Himes books' *If He Hollers Let Him Go,* and *Lonely Crusade*, and examines how Himes candidly mapped Los Angeles and the social relationships that define it. Himes mapped the social relationships of the city within the context of its physical space as well any Angeleno author ever has.

A Narrative as Unwieldly as the City Is

If He Hollers Let Him Go, was chosen by the *LA Weekly* in January 2013 as the greatest Los Angeles novel ever written. Among many positive attributes of the book cited by the Weekly, one of the main reasons they selected it as the penultimate iconic LA work is because "Himes' novel is as unwieldy as this city is." The narrative presented by Himes is set in the wartime Los Angeles of the early 1940s. Published in 1945, the story travels all over southern California to places like the shipyards in San Pedro, the Dunbar Hotel and Lincoln Theater on Central Avenue, a movie palace in Downtown LA, the wealthy African-American district of West Adams and other points in between like Sunset Boulevard and Sepulveda on the Westside of the city.

In each of these sites, the book's African-American protagonist Bob Jones, a shipyard worker, is "relentlessly plagued by the effects of World War II racism." Throughout his movement in the book we observe both the way he is treated in different settings and his interior monologue reacting to the world around him. Early in the book Jones reflects on the Japanese internment camps: "I was the same color as the Japanese and I couldn't tell the difference. 'A yeller-bellied Jap' coulda meant me too. I could always feel race trouble, serious trouble, never more than two feet off. Nobody bothered me. Nobody said a word. But I was tensed every moment to spring." The underlying tension described here by Jones is a guiding theme in the book and it plays out again and again whether it's on the job with his coworkers or he's out at an exclusive restaurant with his fiancé.

A Foreword of the book written in 2002 by the award-winning *New Yorker* staff writer Hilton Als characterizes the story arc as:

> "a portrait of race as an economic and psychosexual prison—or padded cell. The novel takes place over a period of four days, during which its hero, Bob Jones, a shipyard worker in Los Angeles, faces a number of calamities: he is hoodwinked out of his job, framed for a rape, beaten up by white workers, and antagonized by the police. His light-skinned fiancé refuses to help him escape, and Jones's only way out is to join the Army."

Throughout each of these struggles the protagonist reflects on where he is geographically within the city and how the established social relationships are a force larger than he is. In one instance, he recalls being pulled over while driving with his significant other: "We got the traffic ticket just as we were coming into Santa Monica. Two motorcycle cops pulled up and flagged us down. They rolled to a stop in front of us, stormed back on foot, cursing."

Als goes further to say, "that Jones' fear is predicated less on these events than on a fascination with his own marginalization.

While he is concretely persecuted for being black, Jones seems, at times, more affected by the persecution he intuits, by the racism that he observes and absorbs like a dirty sponge." The existential struggle grows bigger and bigger as the story continues. Throughout the book Himes demonstrates an intimate understanding of the unspoken rules which govern each neighborhood whether he's reflecting on a condescending waiter in an exclusive downtown restaurant or the wealthy father of his fiancé in West Adams.

Beyond his insightful narrative and ability to characterize social relationships, another factor that sets Himes apart is his boldness. Both *If He Hollers Let Him Go*, and *Lonely Crusade* contain incisive social criticism that few African-American writers dared to utter during the 1940s. In the early stages of Himes career, he was in the elite company of novelists Ralph Ellison and Richard Wright as an author critiquing race relations in America. By the 1950s and beyond James Baldwin and others carried on this courageous work, but during the late 1940s, Himes set an important precedent with his ability to tell it like it is in terms of racial politics.

Mapping the Social Relationships

Lonely Crusade, picked up the torch from *If He Hollers Let Him Go*. Published in 1947, two years afterwards, this work is twice as long as the earlier book, clocking in at nearly 400 pages. The story is also set in wartime Los Angeles and anchored by a misunderstood young black man protagonist named Lee Gordon. Though *Lonely Crusade*, was not as critically acclaimed as *If He Hollers Let Him Go*, it maps the social relationships and racial politics of the city with the same effectiveness. James Baldwin described it by writing: "Mr. Himes undertakes to consider the ever-present subconscious terror of the black man, the political morality of American Communists, the psychology of union politics, Uncle Tomism, and the relationships between Jews and Blacks. The value of this book lies in its efforts to understand the oppressed and oppressor and their relationship to each other."

Lonely Crusade, visits many of the same places described in *If He Hollers Let Him Go*, like Central Avenue, Downtown Los Angeles and San Pedro, but it also travels to Pasadena, Boyle Heights, City Terrace and Culver City. Like how he does in the earlier work, Himes vividly describes the landscape, underlying racial politics of each area and the existential angst alive during the 1940s. A great example of this can be seen in his characterization of City Terrace: "On both sides were vacant lots also overgrown with weeds. Beyond, going up the hill toward the reservoir, lived Mexicans, and going down towards City Terrace Drive, lived Jews. Several families of white Southern migrants lived on the cutoff circling down behind." In the paragraphs following this, he describes the relations between the groups and how the social climate is shaped by the topography of the neighborhood.

Another example of his powers to capture the landscape, sociology and existential angst from this work includes the Los Angeles River. Himes writes, "At twilight she stood on the Sixth Street Bridge over the Los Angeles River valley, looking down at the railroad tracks. Darkness came and she still stood, and then she found herself walking aimlessly through the city again. Men spoke to her, cars pulled up and slowed, but she did not notice." This passage describes the wife of the protagonist in a moment of despair and how her interaction with the city facilitated her angst. Throughout the book Himes uses the neighborhoods of Los Angeles as accessories to tell the story of race relations and tension in the city.

Furthermore, the dialogue between characters also pulls no punches. In the time of the Cold War and McCarthyism,

Himes was uncensored and wrote about conditions in southern California without sugarcoating anything. Himes will never be accused of wearing rose-colored lenses. In retrospect, it makes sense that *If He Hollers Let Him Go*, is considered one of the greatest LA novels ever. Himes was ahead of his time and captured the spirit of the city with the same critical analysis that John Steinbeck captured California in *The Grapes of Wrath*, and social historians like Carey McWilliams and Mike Davis did in their nonfiction Los Angeles studies. The scholar Stacy Morgan in his book, "Rethinking Social Realism: African American Art and Literature, 1930-1953," considers Himes a pioneer of African-American social realism. Himes' work is also lauded by the critical race studies scholar Frantz Fanon in his classic work, *Black Skin, White Masks*.

By the mid-1950s, Himes moved to France and lived the last three decades of his life there and in Spain where he finally died in 1984. In his later years, he wrote a series of Harlem Detective novels that outsold most of his earlier works, though most critics consider his two LA novels much more powerful and complicated.

As noted in the beginning of this essay, Chester Himes characterizes Los Angeles geographically and racially as well as any writer ever has. These two books are brilliant period pieces that offer crystal clear pictures of wartime southern California. On page after page, neighborhoods and sites are mapped and described with brutal honesty. Himes had a unique ability to both craft a compelling narrative and capture the underlying spirit of the region. Salute to Chester Himes for being one of the greatest novelists to ever write in the landscape of LA Letters.

Luis J. Rodriguez

Luis J. Rodriguez is a love poem to Los Angeles
Under her sky honoring ancestors
In every corner of the metropolis
Singing sonnets for the people

Justice comes to dance with our laureate

Reconciling hungry songs in the shadow
Opening the blast furnace of suburbia
Deconstructing the concrete river
Rodriguez offers in every breath, a prayer
In every poem the gold beneath our feet
Giving the borrowed bones another day
Understand his name's not Rodriguez
Every road he rides is a poem
Zapping us back to a place called home

One for Wanda

For Wanda Coleman (1946-2013)

1.
Hey Wanda! One of the last moves Austin made before
he split the planet: make sure the Ascot Branch
of the Los Angeles Public Library was dedicated to you.
Remember the library you ran to when you needed a place
to escape so long ago. Dozens of your books are now on the
shelf below a framed copy of your *Los Angeles Times* Obituary.

2.
A dozen feet from your section, four tables are set aside
as the student zone for homework help. Black and brown teens
huddle in a circle completing worksheets while a young woman
explained equations. A seventh-grade boy chased his younger
brother while their mother reads a magazine. In 1957, you chased
your dream to be a published author sitting in these chairs.

3.
The librarian can no longer admonish you for staying late. Your
Dreamwalks down Main across San Pedro through Florence-
Firestone set off a landslide of poems bearing witness
to *African Sleeping Sickness*. Apply the *Mercurochrome*,
a young girl sleeps in her mother's arms, the California condor
are gone but your books remain stacked on the west wall. Hear
the footfalls from children down the hall.

4.
You were *A Native in a Strange Land*; you drank a lifetime
of *Bathwater Wine*. Morning after morning, there wasn't a pill
you didn't swallow, *you were in touch beyond clichés, erasing
all the names of the betrayers.* Your crowning glory on the page
channeling blues beyond Broadway: A chorus of cosmic
American Sonnets broadcasting honest-truth. You asked who
will sing your praisesong, I assure you, we are many.
Your resurrection reverberates through the firmament.
We will never forget you Wanda. Ms. Coleman, you
put our city on the map; you made history, *without you
this city, is a pale rude fiction.*

5.
I drove to Florence & Main to say your name.
After visiting your library, I cruised down
San Pedro past Fremont High School.
You said *it's insanity writing poetry
in Los Angeles*, yes this is true, but *something
significant has happened here*, you liberated
a generation of bards sending us down boulevards & avenues
to locate the landscape vernacular.
Poetry alone cannot contain your gravitas.
Driving down Avalon up to 76th Street near
your childhood home, I feel the mercury burning this late
afternoon. I remember your flame-thrower
cocktail of kindness, your uncompromising vision.
Without. You. This city. Is pale. Rude. Fiction.

ODE to LA Women Writers

Let it be known that this place is LA, here the women
attain supreme enlightenment; here the women turn the dharma
wheel, here the women make the city heal—
For over a century, LA women writers have made the city lighter,
our pacifist freedom fighters evoke awakening, patience, generosity,
mercy and compassion like only a woman can—
Forget the natural disasters, LA women writers are the masters
of this ecology, the authorities of civic psychology
forecasting the future of LA reality

Though a fantasy Spanish heritage was concocted by Helen
Hunt Jackson's *Ramona* oppositional intellectual women writers
set the LA story right one narrative at a time

> Leimert Park to Boyle Heights, a Little Tokyo Café
> on Tuesday night, Traci Kato-Kiriyama, Marjorie Light,
> TK Le, Naomi Hirahara, Irene Soriano, Amy Uyematsu,
> Karen Tei Yamashita, Karen Ishizuka publishing in *Gidra*,

LA women writers at Avenue 50 and the Woman's Center
for Creative Work, exchange culture at the Kaleidoscope Kollective,
propose manuscripts at Women Who Submit, sharpen their focus
with La Luna Locas, fight gentrification with Ovarian Psycos.
Pioneers of community based public history redefine the city space
with *The Power of Place*, map unsolved mysteries with
the Studio of Southern California History

> LA Women writers sleep with the dictionary
> > like Harryette Mullen,
> LA Women writers write themselves into the story
> > like Octavia Butler,
> *The Parable of the Sower*, restructuring architecture

of the void like Esther McCoy, travel from Hollywood
to Watts with Wanda Coleman more than the unofficial
poet laureate, beyond Bukowski's sister,
                                there was no one more honest,
                                check her American Sonnets,
Jayne Cortez pioneered the Black Arts Movement,
she grew up in Watts and attended Compton College,
now Compton native Poet Laureate Robin Coste Lewis
carries Cortez's knowledge in a *Voyage of the Sable Venus*
LA Women writers represent East Los Angeles
                                with postmodern prose
                                like Helena Maria Viramontes,
                                the movement is upon us

Behold our divine healers of the word regenerating
LA's spiritual well with poems, plays, short stories, novels
LA women scribes have created a city of their own
rooted in prose and poems, let it be known

        LA Women writers dream a literary life like Carolyn See,
        Dana Johnson connects Inglewood to Moreno Valley,
        redefine LA Noir with Nina Revoyr,
        take a drive to Crenshaw & 54th with Pam Ward
        head to North Long Beach with Liz Gonzalez
        see poetry's heart with S. Pearl Sharpe
        watch Michelle Clinton decipher good sense from the
                faithless,
        attend a poetry festival started by Suzanne Lummis
        get schooled on topics by Jen Hofer or rock
        bilingual poetry workshops with Gloria Alvarez,
        start movements over and over again like Terry Wolverton
        there was no glass ceiling at the Woman's Building,
        only a city of feeling with Eloise Klein Healy,
        Laurel Ann Bogen sings *Psychosis in the Produce Department*
        take a drive with Juniper Song and Steph Cha

Let it be known that this place is LA where
Michele Serros inspired a generation of Chicanas
reunite with elders via Ofelia Esparza,
ride the rails with Marisela Norte,
roll with Lynell George from Evergreen to Culver City
hike all the way up with Teresa Mei-Chuc
get your roots and wings with Jesse Bliss
let Lisa See transport you *On Gold Mountain*
Joan Didion to Erin Aubry Kaplan,
Patti Morrison to Denise Hamilton
Elena Karina Byrne to Carolina Miranda
Wendy Ortiz to Kate Braverman

Central Avenue neon with Natashia Deon
conscious chain reactions with Ashaki Jackson
explore the cosmos with Rocío Carlos,
visit Southeast LA County with Vickie Vertiz,
manifest magic unplanned with Iris DeAnda
keep the word soaring with Gina Loring

Let it be known that this place is LA with women writers in every genre: Jamie Fitzgerald, Myriam Gurba, Phoebe Ozuna, Desiree Zamorano, Zoë Ruiz, Teka Lark, Janice Lee, Gail Wronsky, Ellyn Maybe, Nicelle Davis, Rebecca Gonzalez, Kat Magill, Tamara Blue, Nikki Black, Amelie Frank, Cheryl Klein, Amina Cain, Susan Straight, Melissa Chadburn, Susan Hayden, Alexis Rhone Fancher, Sara Borjas, Marsha de la O

Do you know Sandra Tsing Loh? Luivette Resto, Amy Gerstler, Aimee Bender, Rachel Resnick, V. Kalli, Imani Tolliver, Xochitl Julisa-Bermejo, Linda Albertano, Holly Prado, Yxta Maya Murray, Naomi Quinonez, Nicole Macias, Claudia Rodriguez, Andrea Gutierrez, Carol Muske-Dukes, Judith Freeman, Lynn Thompson, Nicky Schildkraut, E. Amato, Cynthia Guardado, Janet Fitch, Kim Cooper, Olga Garcia,

Jessica Ceballos, Gia Scott-Heron, Rachel Kann, Eve Babitz, Shonda Buchanan

Behold younger voices like Monique Mitchell, Amanda Gorman, Rosalinda Flores, Camille Jácome, Mila Cuda, Blazhia Parker, Stephanie Escobar
LA women writers are only getting started
I see her hair is burning, the hills are filled with fire,
if she said she never loved you, it's you that is the liar

> Let it be known that this place is LA,
>> here the women attain supreme enlightenment;
>> here the women turn the dharma wheel,
>> here the women make the city heal—

A list poem is trouble because it will never be complete, it can never be, for any names you don't see, shout them out, write your own poem, let it be known!

The Legacy of the Woman's Building and How It Lives On

From 1973 to 1991 the Woman's Building was an epicenter of both the Feminist Art Movement and the Los Angeles Community Arts scene. Standing in the elite pantheon of other important and historic L.A. literary spaces like the Watts Writers Workshop, Beyond Baroque, and the World Stage, the Woman's Building not only featured poetry but also showcased visual arts, dance, performance art, film, political activism, graphic design and experimental theater. This essay examines the legacy of the Woman's Building and reveals how the spirit lives on to this day.

Founded in 1973 by artist Judy Chicago, graphic designer Sheila Levrant de Bretteville, and art historian Arlene Raven, the Woman's Building was first located near MacArthur Park in a structure that once housed the old Chouinard Art Institute. The three founders had all been affiliated with the California Institute of the Arts. Together they started the first independent school for women artists, the Feminist Studio Workshop (FSW). They took the inspiration and name for the Woman's Building from a structure built by Sophia Hayden for the 1893 Columbian Exposition in Chicago that displayed exhibitions of cultural works by women from around the world.

Among the hundreds of articles and several dissertations covering the history of the Woman's Building, perhaps the most definitive account is the book *Insurgent Muse*, written by Terry Wolverton and published by City Lights. Wolverton moved to Los Angeles in 1976 to study at the Feminist Studio

Workshop (FSW) and ended up remaining involved in the Woman's Building until 1989. In her own words, she says, "I spent thirteen years—from 1976 to 1989—at the Woman's Building, beginning as a student in the FSW, then becoming a teacher, program director, exhibiting artist, publicist, typesetter, newsletter editor, grant-writer, board member, development director, and eventually executive director."

Wolverton notes in her introduction that, "Rather than attempt a comprehensive history, I've chosen to focus on the activities I was most directly involved and that best illustrate certain premises I want to highlight." Despite this caveat, the book offers an extensive history and a deep examination of the spirit and ethos that defined the monumental site. She begins by discussing the zeitgeist of the early 1970s as the Woman's Building was coming to rise, and why the founders felt it necessary to begin the first independent academy for women artists.

Wolverton notes that the founders, especially de Bretteville, "did not want to replicate another ivory tower, and sought to align this new school with the burgeoning women's movement in Los Angeles." Their hope was to "Push for better inclusion of women in the mainstream art world and the utter redefinition of art and culture within a feminist context." A central thrust within this redefinition was to develop women's artistic identity and sensibility and the expression of these influences through their artwork. To this end, the Woman's Building when it first opened included multiple galleries, theater companies, a coffeehouse, Sisterhood Bookstore, Womantours Travel Agency, and the offices of the National Organization for Women. The idea was to be a one-stop public center for women and their artistic, social and political needs.

In 1975 the Woman's Building moved to a three-story converted red brick warehouse at 1727 North Spring in the liminal stretch where Chinatown and Lincoln Heights meet. Wolverton arrived in Los Angeles shortly after the relocation to study at the Feminist Studio Workshop. In her book, she describes the troubled state of mind she was in before she left the Midwest. Wolverton left Michigan in her early 20s after reading about the Woman's Building in a magazine. Her book's narrative about the era strikes a perfect balance between weaving her own personal history with the collective history of the Woman's Building. Following a failed suicide attempt, she decided to leave behind "the constricted fictions of the Midwest, its constipated possibilities, the cold, the drab, the predictable gaze that would not see you in your full dimensions. You came to put the fragments of your life together, following that spark, to re-knit the woman to the artist, the body to the brain, the spirit."

Over the years of 1973 to 1981, hundreds of women like Wolverton came from not only all over America but all over the world to study at the Feminist Studio Workshop in the Woman's Building. As the years went on the Woman's Building evolved with the times. Wolverton was a central figure in the Lesbian Art Project during the late 1970s. Consisting of a wide range of performance pieces, workshops, and many visual art exhibits, the project "engaged in creating a myth of the lesbian as artist." One of the landmark programs from the period was the 1979 event, "An Oral Herstory of Lesbianism."

In 1981 the Feminist Studio Workshop at the Woman's Building ended, but the space continued and the programming changed to evolve with the times. Wolverton explains that the FSW closing occurred because of "economic shifts and the sea change in social attitudes that followed the election of President Ronald Reagan." Nonetheless the Woman's Building continued until 1991 with art making, exhibitions, and education for women artists. During the 1980s Wolverton was deeply involved with projects there, like the Great American Lesbian Art Show, the Incest Awareness Project, and the White Women's Anti-Racism Consciousness-Raising Group.

Wolverton describes her own evolution as the times changed: "We'd gone from being hippie Outlaw artists to being landlords, business managers, and board members," she says. "I suppose one might say we grew up. For our love of the Woman's Building, our commitment to its vision of feminist art, we entered a world of balance sheets, grantsmanship and marketing. It was a turn of events rich with irony."

Amid all the other programming there were frequent writing workshops and poetry events over the years, featuring many important writers like Deena Metzger, Adrienne Rich, Audre Lorde, Eloise Klein Healy, and Wanda Coleman. Metzger was an important writing mentor for Wolverton. The events were supplemented with the production of literary publication projects, including *Manteniendo El Espiritu*, edited by Aleida Rodriguez, and *Women for All Seasons*, edited by Wanda Coleman.

As the 1980s went on the economic shifts in America made it much more difficult to keep the bills paid. Federal funding for art programming was literally sliced in half. Nonetheless the Woman's Building managed to last all the way until 1991 through a variety of creative means. Wolverton herself remained there until 1989, even acting as the Executive Director towards the end of her time there.

The social conditions of the 1980s caused the zeitgeist emerging from the Woman's Building to shift to a larger picture from the original vision. Wolverton describes how the ethos of the Woman's Building evolved during this time: "Our understanding of oppression grew more sophisticated as we began to perceive patterns and linkages between women, people of color, political exiles, immigrants, poor people, gays and lesbians. Whereas once we might have believed that ending sexism would transform the world, we now saw oppression as a web with many strands that would require alliance, not separatism, to untangle."

With *Insurgent Muse*, Wolverton offers a thorough portrait of the Woman's Building, from its utopian beginnings to the eventual demise. In the book's conclusion, she notes how many of her co-conspirators from the era are now carrying on the work in various locations like public schools, universities, galleries, and writing workshops. "The Woman's Building was at one time like a seedpod," she writes, "where we clustered together, enclosed and safe, as we gathered our potential; then the pod burst open and we were scattered in the wind to sow ourselves in far-flung gardens."

Wolverton herself has gone on to write 12 books of poetry, fiction and creative nonfiction. She has edited 12 other anthologies and mentored hundreds of writers through her various writing workshops and teaching profession at Antioch University. In 1997, she started Writers at Work on Fountain Avenue in Silver Lake, where she carries on the spirit of the Woman's Building with writing classes, frequent workshops, Kundalini Yoga, one-on-one consultation and meditation. Most of all, she "dispenses the medicine of encouragement."

The Leimert Park poet A.K. Toney has known Wolverton since the mid-1990s and been published in a few of her anthologies. "Terry Wolverton is a pioneer in the discipline of poetry," Toney says. "No one has done more for Los Angeles poets in the last 20 years than her, whether she is consulting, writing, creating new forms of poetry or conducting workshops and retreats that help poets refine their craft and get published. She is truly a heroine for the Los Angeles Literary scene." A concrete example of what Toney mentions here is Wolverton's two plus decades of holding writing workshops for writers with HIV. In the early 1990s, she helped the writer Gil Cuadros find his voice and eventually publish his award-winning short stories and poetry. Though Cuadros died of HIV in 1996, his 1994 book *City of God* is still in print and considered by many to be a masterpiece. How time with Wolverton was critical in his devolpment.

The diverse programming offered at Writers at Work has lasted two decades because Wolverton loves to serve the needs of writers. Professor and fiction writer Cheryl Klein says, "If I won the lottery, Terry Wolverton would be one of the first recipients of my personal genius grant fund. She's a true Renaissance woman, in that she produces rich poetry and thought-provoking prose, AND she has an amazingly organized mind that can nail the problems of the publishing world and dissect what's not working about a plot. (She taught me how to plot a novel, which my MFA program failed to.)"

For Wolverton, she credits all that she has become from her years at the Woman's Building, which has taught her "the necessity of space, having territory one can claim, ground in which the community can take root." In the final page of her book she writes, "In the shadow of Dodger Stadium, we discovered the mythic, the sacred, and savored the richness of life that comes from planting oneself in that ground." The legacy of the Woman's Building lives on in spaces like Writers at Work and Antioch College, where Eloise Klein Healy founded her progressive MFA writing program. Similarly, one of the founders of the Woman's Building, Sheila de Bretteville, has created several public art projects honoring the lives of women such as Biddy Mason State Park in Downtown Los Angeles.

Wolverton acknowledges that there were more events, exhibits and remarkable women participating at the Woman's Building than she could ever possibly name in one book; nonetheless she captures the powerful spirit that emerged from the site and does an excellent job explaining why it was so important and how it still lives on. Salute to Terry Wolverton and the hundreds of women who participated at the Woman's Building; they are all queens in the landscape of L.A. Letters.

Remembering Michele Serros

When I first entered the spoken word and writing community in the mid-1990s, one of the biggest names in the Southern California scene was Michele Serros. The Oxnard-born Serros was a groundbreaking Chicana poet, essayist, novelist, and comedic writer. Serros passed on January 5, 2015 at the age of 48 after a long battle with cancer. This essay remembers her legacy and shares memories of Serros and her work from a longtime friend and many of her admirers. A number of poets gathered in Los Angeles in El Sereno at the Here & Now space on Huntington Drive to celebrate Serros on Sunday, January 11 in an event organized by Catherine Uribe-Abee, Steve Abee, and Iris DeAnda. Steve Abee called her the "California punk rock surfer girl genius speaking the truth for us all."

There was also a large event in Berkeley a few days before that. Over the first two weeks of January 2015, the social media feed in both the Southern and Northern California writing communities were filled with testimonials about the power of her work as well as her compassionate personality. Before sharing some of these tributes, it's important to highlight her many literary accomplishments.

Serros began writing in her teen years and had her first book published while still attending Santa Monica College, before she transferred to UCLA. The book, *Chicana Falsa and other stories of Death, Identity and Oxnard*, was originally published by the small publisher, Lalo Press in 1994. Around this time Serros began performing her work all over Southern California and quickly made a name for herself with her potent work and charismatic reading style. She made such an impression that

Rage Against the Machine featured the book's cover in one of their album's liner notes.

Following the buzz around her writing and her book, Serros was chosen as one of the 12 poets to be featured in Lollapalooza in stages across the country. One of the voices who traveled with her for the Las Vegas leg of the Lollapalooza tour was the prominent Leimert Park novelist and poet, Pam Ward. Ward told me, "Michelle would skateboard around the parking lot of the arena. Michele was big time and I remember her making the sea of people, which was thousands, at this first time event laugh. It was amazing!"

Serros was so compelling on the Lollapalooza tour that Billy Corgan from Smashing Pumpkins accompanied her on bass guitar a number of times for the piece, "Mr. Boom Boom Man." When she finished touring Lollapalooza, Mouth Almighty Records asked Serros to record her work and in 1996, they released a spoken word recording of *Chicana Falsa*.

The success of Chicana Falsa, as both an independent book and spoken word album, led Riverhead Books, a much bigger publisher, to pick it up and republish it for a national audience in 1998. Riverhead is a subsidiary of Penguin/Putnam and this new development brought even more attention to Serros's work across America. Newsweek Magazine called her "A Woman to Watch in the New Century."

The accolades continued in the year 2000 when she published a book of short stories, *How to Be a Chicana Role Model,* which became a *Los Angeles Times* Bestseller. Flea from the Red Hot Chili Peppers lauded the book in an interview around this time, praising her mix of humor and poignancy. Serros moved to New York City in 2001 and began to tour even more at book fairs and schools across the country.

In 2002, Serros was hired by George Lopez and ABC to write for his television sitcom, even though she had never written a screenplay or done any writing for television previously. As the year went on, Serros continued to tour as a motivational speaker at universities, organizations, and museums across America. In addition to speaking at a Stanford University Commencement in 2002, she began to record pieces for National Public Radio and other news outlets. During the same year, she also read her work at the Lincoln Center for the Performing Arts, sharing the stage with luminaries like Studs Terkel, George Plimpton, and Arthur Miller. In 2006 and 2007, Serros wrote two young adult novels, *Honey Blonde Chica*, and *!Scandalosa!,* which were published by the SimonPulse branch of Simon and Schuster.

Beyond her extensive writing credits, Michele Serros is remembered for inspiring thousands of young writers and by her colleagues for her brilliant sense of humor. As noted above, Pam Ward shared the stage with Serros at Lollapalooza, and she told me several anecdotes about their close friendship and several years of collaborating. "Michele and I met at the Beyond Baroque Literary Arts Foundation. We were in a woman's poetry workshop run by Michelle T. Clinton, who was a powerful force in the literary community during the 80s-90s," Ward says. "With Nancy Agabian, Maria Cabildo, and Michele Serros, we formed a poetry troupe called 'Guava Breasts' which performed all over L.A. Maria was the founder of the group. Nancy Agabian would do things like crochet a penis on stage. It was like performance meets poetry. We had so much fun. We were kind of like S.A. Griffin's Carma Bums with Nancy Sinatra clothes."

Ward has many fond memories of their dozens of readings together. She says, "We would throw tampons out at the audience with poetry lines written on them, and would always feature a cool girl writer to read with us. I was on Michele's CD *Chicana Falsa*. She was a great writer who bravely articulated her own voice and stuck to her guns in the true vein of authenticity. What was unique about Michele and all of us was the way we would incorporate vivid humor to illustrate hard topics. You could not come to a 'Guava Breast' show and not laugh. That was Michele's true gift. She was an honest, brilliant poet who could tell a funny story about the food section in a store and really make a political statement." This piece Ward mentions, "Attention Shoppers," is one of Serros's best known works.

Ward also remembers Serros for her unique fashion sense. "She loved to dress in go-go boots and rock short shirts and with a voice that sounded like Rocky in 'Rocky and Bullwinkle.' She was one in a million," Ward says. "She was all of these contradictions, a Mexican chick who surfed, and a bookworm who donned go-go boots and also loved Judy Bloom." Ward also remembers that Michelle created a T-shirt line called "Medium Brown Girl" based on the Bloomingdales Medium Brown bag. "She sold a ton of those to women of medium brown everywhere. My daughters wore theirs proudly."

The award-winning Chicana poet and educator Xochitl-Julisa Bermejo told me about the huge influence Serros had on her work. "I think I was in my mid-20s probably living at my parents' when I found the Michele Serros book, *How to Be a Chicana Role Model*, among my mom's Chicana Studies textbooks and started reading it," Bermejo writes. "I remember feeling like it was a guidebook written just for me ... I remember a scene in 'How to be a Chicana Role Model' where copies of Michele's poetry collection doubled as a coffee table. That was first time I saw someone like me doing what I wanted to do." Bermejo adds, "Farewell, Michele. Thank you for being a Chicana role model that showed me I could be a writer if I wanted."

Another Chicano on whom Serros had a major influence is the bookstore owner and interdisciplinary scholar, Frank Sosa. Sosa owned Thirty Three and a Third Books in Echo Park from

2000 to 2006, where he proudly sold her books and the spoken word album. He recently told me, "I came across 'Chicana Falsa' in 1995 or 1996. I was just becoming politicized at the time, and to be honest I wasn't well-read either. I was 23 years old. The book was critical for this mono-lingual (a problem Serros brilliantly tackles in "Mi Problema") Chicano from the surf town of Santa Cruz who was trying to make his way in the big city. Here was a voice that spoke of my conundrum of never truly belonging to one community, yet it staked a claim with a powerful, seductive humor. Who could better reach me with titles like 'Mr. Boom Boom Man,' 'La Letty,' 'Annie Says,' and of course, 'Attention Shoppers?' If you haven't heard the Spoken Word CD version of this, the reading is piss in your pants hilarious and if you ever made it to my apartment around that time I might have forced you to listen to it. Michele Serros left us too soon but her legacy will live on."

Another quality Serros was known for was her generous spirit. She moved to Berkeley, California about a half decade ago and married the noted chef, Antonio Magana. Magana owns and operates Flacos Tacos, a famous Mexican Vegan eatery in Berkeley. Frank Sosa also now lives in Berkeley, and he told me that his daughter goes to a dual immersion preschool in Berkeley called Centro Vida and that Flacos always supports the school's fundraising efforts. "They donated enough masa last year to make over 5000 tamales for our annual fundraiser," he says.

Over the last week there were many other similar stories shared on Facebook and Twitter about the veracity of Serros's work and her generous spirit. A public church service for Michele Serros was held January 24, 2015 at Santa Clara Church in Oxnard, California.

A final word about her legacy comes from Pam Ward, "I mean this chick published young and went on to read at the Lincoln Center with Arthur Miller! She was way ahead of her time and

I will never forget her." Salute to Michele Serros for brilliant literary work and powerful spirit. She will always be a queen of California and L.A. Letters.

Tonalli Studio: The Spark of Creation in the Land of WE

Tonalli Studio is an artistic space located on Avenida Cesar Chavez in the middle of the Maravilla district of East Los Angeles. Founded by Ofelia Esparza and her daughter Rosanna Esparza Ahrens in January 2012, their space is both a gallery and retail boutique. Moreover, it is a meeting place for the healthy and creative community to convene through art exhibits, poetry, music, yoga, wellness workshops and community building.

"Come on in, our space is for everyone," says Ofelia Esparza. The 85-year-old Esparza is a lifelong resident of the Belvedere section of East Los Angeles and can rightfully be called one of the matriarchs of the Eastside art community. Esparza is internationally known for the exquisite altars that she makes. They have been shown in galleries and museums all over the world. Her altars first received acclaim at Self Help Graphics in the late 1970s. Her life-story is one for the ages and you can sense her kindness, wisdom and knowledge when she speaks.

Tomas Benitez was the longtime Executive Director of Self Help Graphics and he says, "Because of her striking shock of white hair and deep-set beautiful eyes, Ofelia was often mistaken for a holy woman. Not such a mistake because she has been a spiritual leader in our hearts for a while now. I thank her for infusing my soul with the true meaning of Día de los Muertos, of the spiritual ritual in art making, going back to the very root of the practice."

Ofelia's daughter Rosanna is their in-house designer and she corroborates with Benitez when she says, "Working with my mother is like witnessing a day unfold. She is elegant, kind and full of grace for everyone. I have a long way to go to be like her. Every day I am amazed at her stamina and her vision for the future. She is 85 and feels there is still so much she wants to accomplish."

Ofelia Esparza never set out to become an internationally known artist, but it slowly manifested as time unfolded. Four major testimonies to her influence over the last year include Cal State Los Angeles awarding her an honorary Ph.D. in Humane Letters, Tia Chucha's Café Centro Cultural awarding her a lifetime achievement award in 2016 and her high school alma mater, Garfield honoring her in their Hall of Fame as a distinguished alumnus. The latest honor is a huge mural of her face recently painted and completed on the western outside wall of Tonalli Studio by the celebrated artist Erin Yoshi.

The Spirit of Chicano Art & Culture

Esparza originally began Working with Self Help Graphics during the 1970s by helping with their workshops for Día de Los Muertos. Gradually her skills with altar-making were so exemplary that she became one of their featured altar makers for the annual Día de Los Muertos events and other events in the space. "When you hear her talk about art, you hear joy in her voice," says Benitez. "She isn't so much an artist as she is an art maker, and you can see the sheer joy she has in process as she moves about, and in her voice as she casually talks about what she is doing. She is the spirit of Chicano art and culture to me."

Esparza taught at City Terrace Elementary School for 28 years and grew up in a creative environment. Looking back, she says that though the people that were around her as she was growing up never called themselves artists, that's exactly what they were. "My mother never opened a can of food in her life. She grew all of her own vegetables or if she did not grow it herself, she bartered with local vendors or neighbors to get the produce she wanted," Esparza recalls. She has fond memories of her mother's resourcefulness. "I never knew we were poor," she says, "because my mother was so resourceful." She grew up surrounded by people, good food, music and lively conversation. She recalls that all her neighbors and people around her family were artisans. "They were people always making something out of nothing," she says. Her family's resourcefulness grounded her from a very early age. During junior high she also became inspired by the artwork of painter and muralist Charles White and his "Images of Dignity" series. White's refined style of honoring the common person resonated with Esparza, and the spirit of celebrating people's dignity is a core concept that she retained for her own creative work.

Esparza gave birth to nine children and was married for many years before her husband passed a few decades ago. Her husband was a truck driver and was skilled at making things. He was always creating things around their house to make their family's life better. She went back to school in 1967 after her children were raised and began her teaching career in her 40s after receiving her Bachelor's degree and then Teaching Credential in 1974-75.

Sharon Sekhon, the Founder of the Studio of Southern California History says: "Ofelia Esparza has shared her history with the Studio for Southern California History. When she tells us our history, Ofelia does it in a way that is touchable and accessible. She is a tether to our better selves and our better America."

Sekhon first met Esparza through Tomas Benitez. Sekhon is also a big supporter of Tonalli Studio. She says that people congregate there because it is an extension of Ofelia Esparza.

"Tonalli is a safe space to be," says Sekhon. "Whether it is just a casual visit with Ofelia, or through holistic workshops, or the unparalleled exhibits they hold with masterpiece art from voices we do not hear ever acknowledged in Los Angeles now but will be collected once we are dead. Ofelia advocates for her community in ways that we may all benefit- her door is open if you have an open heart." The space also includes a boutique selling women's apparel, incense, body oils, books and eclectic artful accessories.

The Spark of Creation

During June and July of 2017, I visited Tonalli Studio on several occasions. With each visit, I learned more and more about Ofelia Esparza, their gallery, her practice, the surrounding neighborhood and the incredible depth which grounds the entire space. To begin, "Tonalli," is a word with roots in Mesoamerica which means, "that which creates or emanates energy; or, the spark of creation." Analogous to chi and spiritual energy, Esparza chose this word for their space after seeing it in one of her many reference books. The idea of their space being a site for the spark of creation resonated with both Ofelia and Rosanna and fit their intentions perfectly.

Another interesting point of discussion Esparza shared was regarding the geography of the local neighborhood where Tonalli is located. This stretch of Cesar Chavez where the space exists is just east of the 710 and is a district known by locals as Old Town Maravilla. Most Angelenos that do not know the specifics of this section of the Eastside just call it all East LA, but they do not realize that East LA is a separate area from Boyle Heights and that there are sections of Unincorporated East LA such as City Terrace, Belvedere and Maravilla.

Residents of South Los Angeles can relate to this compression the way some attempt to lump Inglewood, Watts, Compton and Crenshaw all together, when they are indeed each separate neighborhoods. Belvedere is the section west of the 710 and east of Boyle Heights and City Terrace is the hills just north of Belvedere and Boyle Heights. To further add to the confusion, Belvedere Park is in Maravilla next to East LA College despite being named after Belvedere. Moreover, the park itself was once called Soledad Park before it was renamed. Esparza has lived her entire life between Belvedere and Maravilla and she taught in City Terrace for 28 years. She told me that in many ways the areas overlap, but there are unique elements of each that differentiate them. She loves the area and will always remain loyal. Many of her former students come by the studio, and this always brings her great joy as well. On a few occasions visitors to their space have said, "the gallery and store are so beautiful, why don't you go to Pasadena?" Esparza always tells them that, "We love right where we are and don't want to be anywhere else but here."

Eyes of God

On one of the days I was there speaking to Ofelia Esparza, she was making 50 small "Ojos de Dios" or "eyes of God," as they are called in English for an altar she is making for an upcoming exhibit at the National Museum of Mexican Art in Chicago. Watching her create these objects was spellbinding. Composed of two short sticks bound by bright colored yarn, these decorative ornaments will adorn her altar to represent the souls that have been sacrificed by big business because they were defending the Earth from copper mining, oil drilling, water pollution and deforestation.

She tells me that her altar under construction will be titled "Defenders of Mother Earth," and it is dedicated to the activists around the world that have recently died trying to protect the environment from the above-named processes in places like Honduras, the Amazon and Southern Mexico. She knows of at least 81 deaths in the last few years. She tells me that we do not always hear about these deaths because they are covered up quickly, but that they are continuing more and more as environmental issues escalate. Esparza likes to use branches and twigs as the sticks she wraps the yarn around for each of her Ojos de Dios. She loves employing nature and its grounding influence, especially with an object as sacred as an altar. Her Ojos de Dios are an offering of spirit, health, good fortune and they also represent "the cosmic movement of the earth."

Esparza loves to pass on the act of altar making. She sees it as a sacred act and something she can do to make a difference. She believes—like many—that humans suffer three deaths. "The first is when someone physically dies, the second when a body is laid to rest at the funeral and the third when people stop talking about the person and their spirit is finally forgotten," she shares. Esparza sees the act of altar making as a process which honors people prolonging their memory and acts as a bridge between the waking world and spiritual world.

For the last three decades, Esparza has travelled all over the world making altars. Benitez shared an experience about a time she travelled to Glasgow, Scotland. "We sent her to Glasgow in 1996," Benitez recalls, "as part of a cultural exchange with the Glasgow Print Studio, and she installed their first Day of the Dead (DOD) altar for their first DOD. She was there for a week, left behind her shoes, a pair of glasses, a scarf and lord knows what else." She left such an impression on the studio in Glasgow, Benitez says, that "they took her things and put them in a niche, a decorated box, and her artifacts are still on display in their offices to this day."

The Land of WE

On July 8th, 2017, the Tonalli Studio gallery featured an opening of painter and muralist Erin Yoshi's "The Land of WE."

This collection of paintings from the creative imagination of Yoshi is topped off by a huge mural of Ofelia Esparza on the space's outside western wall. Yoshi's mural celebrates Esparza beautifully with three birds around her face.

This show is also a sort of homecoming because the Monterey Park-born Yoshi grew up in Montebello and East Los Angeles. Yoshi has been in Ecuador for the last few years and she has painted murals across the United States and in The Netherlands, France, Spain, Mexico, Guatemala, Nicaragua, Honduras, Colombia, Ecuador, Chile, Australia, the Philippines and the United Kingdom. Despite all her international accolades, this is her first solo show. For it to be at Tonalli in the same area where she grew up is especially meaningful.

The exhibit spotlights ancient cultural traditions and eco-diversity. WE is a fictional world she's created that "is a land rich in nature and exists pre-climate change." Her work is based in historic cultural memories and informed by current environmental conditions. In a press release describing her artistic process she says, "with signs of global warming starting to appear, I find myself clinging to the natural world from rainforests to underwater canyons." Many of the canvasses within the space are quite large and the subjects include elephants, rare birds and other endangered species Yoshi encountered through her travels.

Yoshi's themes overlap beautifully with Ofelia Esparza and the spirit of Tonalli Studio. The art historian and curator Isabel Rojas-Williams says: "It seems fit that Erin Yoshi's artworks would be part of a beloved East Los Angeles art institution, Tonalli Studio, led by the spiritual altar master Maestra Ofelia Esparza. Yoshi's artworks speak of social justice and class struggles within communities, whether in the U.S. or globally. Her artworks, part of "The Land of We," at Tonalli Studio (July 8th- 2017), reflect her deeply rooted connection with ancient cultural traditions. Yoshi's figurative storytelling directly connects with Ofelia Esparza's spirituality and life-long dedication to social justice."

I briefly met Yoshi in the gallery during the exhibit's first week, and she told me she was thrilled to have her first solo show at Tonalli and with the opportunity to honor Ofelia Esparza in a mural. "The inspiration of the mural is to highlight Ofelia Esparza," she says, "but also it reflects the beauty from within. As one cares, less about the perception of the external world, their light shines brighter. They shed false self-images to reveal their truth. It cherishes the wisdom that comes with age, and celebrates the knowledge that is passed down to future generations. The mural also celebrates the connection we have to the animal world and the environment. It's a glance into 'The Land of WE.'"

Yoshi's description of each painting includes facts and details about the current condition of each subject. Yoshi has an MBA in International Sustainability and her knowledge in this field empowers and imbues her work with that much more meaning. In her artist statement she says, "In a time that places value on newness and technology, where the landscapes are made to be homogenous and sterile, white walls are prioritized over color, I find myself craving that which is historic, natural and being transformed by human disregard and ravenous consumption." Yoshi's collection of paintings in "The Land of WE," and her mural of Ofelia Esparza celebrate beauty, knowledge and wisdom. Yoshi's oeuvre of color combined with the collective work of Ofelia Esparza altars' and the collective Tonalli Studio space all work in lockstep with each other to present an alternative reality that "highlight(s) true beauty," Yoshi says, "and raw emotions within humanity, while capturing the breath that connects us together."

Tonalli Studio is indeed "The Land of WE," in more ways than one. It is a family-run art space created for the community. The work that begins in their space continues across Southern

California and beyond. Ofelia Esparza and her daughter Rosanna have a powerful and symbiotic relationship. "I am inspired by her process," confesses Rosanna. "I'm a procrastinator and she is a planner. She works in stages—methodical—I am constantly learning from her and vice versa. I am more impulsive and a risk taker so this journey as business partners is truly and adventure for both of us."

The familial partnership is further extended because they are also joined in their efforts by other family members like the Herbalist Elena Esparza and performance artist Erendira Bernal. Ofelia also told me that her son helped with a lot of the carpentry, woodwork and various elements constructed within the space over the last five years. One of her other sons makes altars in Pomona and carries on his mother's work with schools in the Inland Empire. This combination of community and creativity epitomizes the dynamic spark of energy that is Tonalli Studio. Rosanna explains, "Our intention is to hold space—a peaceful creative space for the community to come and behold the beautiful that emerges from our culture in all its forms."

Garvey Avenue from Alhambra to El Monte

The San Gabriel Valley (SGV) is very famous for its multicultural mix in cities like Alhambra, Monterey Park and Rosemead. There are several key arteries that connect the web of municipalities in the area. One of the main streets of the SGV that exemplifies its diverse demographics as well as the many different land uses and agrarian history is Garvey Avenue. This essay examines the vibrant landscape along Garvey from Alhambra to El Monte passing through Monterey Park, Rosemead and South El Monte before the main stretch of it flows into the 10 East in El Monte just west of the 605 and Baldwin Park.

Before describing the geographic and streetscape features along Garvey, a brief background history dating back to the late 19th Century is needed. The street is named for Richard Garvey, Sr. Garvey was a mail rider for the United States Government between 1860 and 1863. He delivered mail by horseback across a 300 mile stretch between Arizona and California. Through his travels he discovered that the path that is now Garvey Avenue was the shortest route between El Monte and Los Angeles. He gradually began to love this stretch of land and in 1873, he bought a ranch that was about four miles long and two miles wide. The west end of his ranch was where Atlantic Boulevard is now and the eastern end is where San Gabriel Boulevard is. Most of Garvey's land is now considered Monterey Park and some of it is Rosemead and South San Gabriel.

He gave some of his land to create the east-west highway now called Garvey Avenue. The site of Garvey's ranch house is now called Garvey Ranch Park and is less than a mile south of Garvey and just east of Garfield. Remnants of his home remain on the park as well as an observatory built by his son in the 1930s. The Monterey Park Historical Society has a small museum here and has much more information on both Garvey and the area's early history. In the early 20th Century, long before the construction of Interstate 10, the 60 and 210, Garvey was one of the main routes into Los Angeles. Valley Boulevard was equally important and was originally the path of the Butterfield Stage Coach in the 19th Century.

Valley and Garvey are parallel roads that are related like Pico and Olympic or Wilshire and Santa Monica Boulevard. Both Garvey and Valley run parallel to the 10 and are never more than about a mile apart from each other with the 10 in between the two and like Wilshire and Santa Monica, they also intersect at one point. Garvey and Valley meet in El Monte, just west of where Garvey's main stretch becomes Interstate 10.

The Roads Were the Highways

Garvey Avenue begins in Alhambra just south of the 10 Freeway and Cal State Los Angeles. It officially starts from the curve where Ramona Boulevard splits adjacent to the 10. Residents from Alhambra, Monterey Park and Rosemead often use this stretch of Garvey rather than taking the 10 because the 10 east always slows down just past City Terrace when it reaches Alhambra and Monterey Park by the Fremont exit. For this reason, commuters in the know exit from the 10 on Ramona and when you make a left turn onto Ramona, it becomes Garvey in less than a half mile.

On the western edge of Garvey where it begins, is the Chinese Church for Christ, also called the Calvin Chao Theological Seminary. A few hundred yards east of the church on the northern side of Garvey are three still-functioning archaic roadside hotels that date back to the first half of the 20th Century. They are the Wayfare Motel, Midwick Motor Hotel and the View Motel. All along Garvey heading east are other similar motels that date back over a half century ago. These motels are a lot like the small hotels along Route 66 and other major roads that were once considered highways before the Interstate system was built in the 1950s and early 1960s.

Heading east on this part of Garvey the road curves and heads up hill. This vantage point offers excellent views of Mt. Wilson, Mt. Baldy, and Pasadena to the north and the entire San Gabriel Valley on the eastern horizon. On a clear day, one can even see the towering Mt. San Gorgonio over 50 miles east. The series of foothills in this area are where Alhambra and Monterey Park meet on the western edge. As noted above, the road is fast through this stretch and much like a highway all the way to Atlantic about a mile east.

Coming down Garvey through this area one cannot help but notice the opulent St. Stevens Serbian Orthodox Cathedral on the northern side of Garvey. As one of the largest Orthodox cathedrals in America, the Byzantine architecture of the church is truly awe-inspiring. The location was chosen for its hilltop location and the outstanding view it offers of the San Gabriel Valley below. The Serbian population in the local area was much bigger in the past, nonetheless Serbians and devoted members of the church commute there from all over Southern California.

One of the First Truck Stops

As Garvey descends the hill there is an intersection that crosses with both Fremont and Monterey Pass Road. Monterey Pass Road was once called Coyote Pass for the many coyotes that could be found in the area. Splitting off from Garvey, it heads southwest towards East Los Angeles and City Terrace. Numerous historians have recounted that the Spanish explorer Portola and Father Junipero Serra travelled along Monterey Pass Road on their way to building the second mission in California, which eventually was in San Gabriel. Monterey Pass Road is on the flat stretch between the hills of Monterey Park and City Terrace.

Further down the hill heading east on Garvey, the retail stretch of Monterey Park begins at Atlantic Boulevard. Atlantic was once called Wilson Avenue, named after Don Benito Wilson, the second mayor of Los Angeles in the mid-19th Century and longtime owner of much of the land in the western stretch of the San Gabriel Valley. On the northeastern corner of Garvey and Atlantic sits a vacant gas station that was once a service station owned by Laura Scudders. Scudders started her Potato Chip empire on this very corner in the 1920s. Her family owned the service station there and decided to start selling food items because so many travelers would stop at their station after passing by on Garvey. An exhibit in the Monterey Park Historical Museum noted that many cars broke down along this stretch of Garvey, especially those coming down the hill from what was then Coyote Pass. Scudders created her potato chips and other food items to feed travelers who stopped at the station. Her station was also one of the first rest stops and more extravagant stations like the modern-day truck stops more common these days. A plaque commemorating Scudders sits on the corner and can be seen by pedestrians who look close enough.

East of Atlantic along Garvey, it gradually becomes Downtown Monterey Park. Monterey Park is famous for its large Chinese population. There are more Chinese eateries than one can count. Near Ynez and Garvey is one of the more popular restaurants, Mama Lu's Dumpling House. Further east before Garfield is the Hong Kong Café. Along the way there are Chinese herb shops, teahouses and many other small retail stores. Further down, Yama's Body shop is still open and its one of the last vestiges of Monterey Park's Japanese-American history. Near

Yama's, the eatery known as Victory is a French Vietnamese restaurant. Furthermore, east of Garfield along Garvey are a few locations that date back to the early Anglo history of Monterey Park. Two of these sites are Johnny Thompson's Guitar and Divine's Furniture. Dating back to 1932, Divine's has been an antique furniture store that originally opened by Harry Divine back during the Great Depression. They are widely known in the San Gabriel Valley for great deals and quality merchandise. Their website reports that their building was originally built in 1922 as an open-air Japanese produce market.

Past Divine's and New Avenue, Garvey enters Rosemead. As much as Monterey Park is Chinese, Rosemead is both Chinese and Vietnamese. More than a half dozen Pho eateries are along Garvey as the road heads east through Rosemead into South El Monte and El Monte. The western stretch of Garvey through Rosemead was once an Unincorporated Los Angeles County territory called Wilmar, named after a place in Arkansas. Many of the early residents of Wilmar were from Arkansas and they named the area after their home state not only because they were from Arkansas but because the hills just south of Garvey reminded them of all the hills around their home in Wilmar, Arkansas. Most of the Unincorporated Wilmar territory was eventually annexed into Rosemead about 50 years ago and some of it became a part of South San Gabriel, which remains Unincorporated.

Always Running Down Garvey

Along the southern side of Garvey in Rosemead is Richard Garvey Intermediate School. Los Angeles Poet Laureate Luis Rodriguez grew up in nearby South San Gabriel and writes about the school and his childhood in the area in his memoir *Always Running*. He attended Garvey in the late 1960s. He also reports that there were still a few of the Arkansas descendants in the area during his youth there. Rodriguez devotes a few pages in his book to his years at Garvey. The school is now much better than it was then. Rodriguez describes the conditions when he attended: "We drove teachers nuts at Garvey. A number of them were sent home with nervous breakdowns." Rodriguez's book paints a vivid picture of both the school and the evolving landscape around Rosemead and South San Gabriel as it was over four decades ago.

Local historian and Cal State Los Angeles graduate student in History, Brian Sun also attended Garvey. Sun attended Garvey in the 1990s and has lived most of his life in Monterey Park and Rosemead. Sun has eaten in most of the eateries along Garvey and is an expert in the history of the San Gabriel Valley. He tells me that Rosemead is home to many Southern Chinese and Vietnamese. He recently took me to an indoor mall at Garvey and San Gabriel Boulevard with dozens of restaurants inside called "the Square." The mall that is now "The Square," was once a hardware store called Builder's Square over two decades ago. Sun explains more about the space, "It's an Asian market with a food court. Harlem's Kitchen is the well-known spot for wonton soup and chow fun, they have very authentic Hong Kong food."

At the southwestern corner of Garvey and San Gabriel, near Harlem's Kitchen and the Square is an iconic bell signifying El Camino Real, the road connecting all the California missions. A small concrete bridge a few yards north of the bell reads "1935." The bridge was built over the Alhambra Wash, a small diagonal waterway that connects with the Rio Hondo River a mile south near the Whittier Narrows where Rosemead meets South El Monte.

Continuing east along Garvey there are not only used car lots, small motels, Pho eateries, Vietnamese markets and places offering acupuncture, there are a few trailer and mobile home parks that harken back to Garvey's early history. The Vagabond Villa Trailer Park is one of them. These trailer parks and the few small motels are remaining bits of Appalachia in the cosmopolitan and multicultural milieu that is the 21st century San Gabriel Valley. Streets like Walnut Grove also pay homage to the early agricultural history of the SGV.

There are a few vacant lots along Garvey through Rosemead. Heading east, Garvey briefly enters South El Monte, the self-proclaimed "City of Achievement." South El Monte and El Monte have both had longstanding ties with the Mexican community, but they are also now having a gradual influx of Vietnamese and Chinese residents as well. In the early 20th Century, these communities also had many Japanese-Americans. Amid botanicas, taquerias and Mexican markets there are a few Chinese and Vietnamese markets and bakeries like Mr. Baguette.

On the corner of Garvey and Humbert in South El Monte, there are two Pho eateries directly across from each other. Near Tyler and Garvey in El Monte there is a Boxing and Mixed Martial Arts Gym. The sign in the window says, "Home of the Aztec Dragons." West of Santa Anita on Garvey is King Taco. The mix of Mexican and Asian residents in El Monte and South El Monte corroborate with the thesis espoused by author Wendy Cheng in her book, *The Chang's Next Door to the Diazes*.

Garvey intersects with Valley in El Monte a few blocks east of Peck Road. A few streets east of Valley, Garvey merges with Interstate 10 just past Durfee and starts and stops as a frontage road along the 10 through Baldwin Park and West Covina. The core stretch of Garvey is the 10 miles between Alhambra and El Monte. Valley continues east uninterrupted into the San Gabriel Valley into Baldwin Park, City of Industry, La Puente, Walnut and eventually becomes Holt Avenue in Pomona. Valley extends for over 25 miles and is more known than Garvey. Nonetheless the 10 miles of Garvey between Alhambra and El Monte packs a lot of culture and history in a very concentrated stretch.

There are few streets in Southern California that show the past, present and future of the state like Garvey Avenue. There are many more locations along Garvey than can ever be recounted in one essay. Take a trip down Garvey between Alhambra and El Monte to witness a touchstone slice of geography in the landscape of L.A. Letters.

The Cascades

One hot summer evening in 1999 Phil and I left our apartment in West L.A. with no destination in mind. We headed east on the 10 from the Westside. The setting sun dipped behind our backs as we drove east through the heart of inner-city Los Angeles. Rows of palms sway in the breeze; twilight colors in the sky, Roots album *Illadelphhalflife* pushing us forward. We were glad to get out of the stuffy apartment.

Downtown's towers shined bright just north in front of us as we drove. After passing downtown into East LA, we hit the point the 10 east becomes the 60 East if you stay right. We stayed on the 60 a few stops before exiting Atlantic. There was no plan, we just felt like exploring. These drives are intuitive. I turned left on Atlantic, heading north into Monterey Park.

A few minutes later while heading north on Atlantic feeling the road, we notice on our left side a park with a well-lit hillside waterfall fountain. Quickly I turned left heading towards what looks to be a park. Driving a half block west, it looked like a mirage.

This park appears like Shangri-La out of nowhere. We saw an exquisite waterfall cascading down a hill. The waterfall paved in opulent poured concrete, art deco era, late 1920s flair. The hillside grass frames the waterfall in the middle and large houses sit on both sides of the park. About the size of a park you'd imagine in San Francisco, truly a slice of paradise.

On this particular night, the 300-foot long waterfall running through the slope of the park was glowing bright in the early night. All the lights were on in the waterfall system. We parked the car and got out. Walking up the hill to the top of the park, Phil and were enchanted by the park and its charming waterfall. Finding this location randomly made it even more impressive. We discovered that the park is called the Cascades.

The Cascades were built in 1928 when Monterey Park began developing. A collection of upscale houses in the late 1920s called Midwick View Estates was designed to be on par with Beverly Hills and the Cascades Park was the bait to lure would-be homeowners to Monterey Park and more specifically Midwick View Estates. An outdoor theater like the Hollywood Bowl was set to be built just east of the Cascades.

The Great Depression hit in 1929 and the bigger plans were scrapped. The land open for the outdoor amphitheater is now a small valley dotted with houses just east of Atlantic. From the Cascades, you can see how the local topography of Monterey Park made a perfect site to locate an outdoor venue.

Five years after my first encounter with the Cascades I met my future wife Emi. A week after we started spending time together we drove past the Cascades. I then realized it was the same park Phil and I stumbled on a few years before. It just so happens that the Cascades are a few blocks away from her place. This is when I found out the history of Midwick View Estates, the outdoor theater and why they first built the Cascades.

A few years after this, I ended up moving in with Emi. As the years have gone on, I have walked countless times over to the Cascades to enjoy the sloping hill, the large fountain and pristine view from the top of the park. Most recently, I have spent many afternoons there with our daughter and son as they run down the hill or attempt to put their feet in the fountain. I knew there was something truly extraordinary about the Cascades from the very first time I saw it.

The 626

An abundant landscape of locations, people and culture
exist in the 626. The Crown City in this multicultural
mix is undoubtedly Pasadena. A century ago, citrus groves
stretched from Redlands to Azusa. This was decades before
tract homes were built in Temple City and Covina. The
agricultural scenery was gradually decimated by freeways. Three
centuries earlier the Spanish built the mission in San Gabriel.

The Pueblo of Los Angeles was founded a decade after
the Padres built San Gabriel. Spanish colonization created
the foundation for LA and the future 626. Never in their
wildest dreams did the Franciscans envision freeways.
During the Victorian era, old money Yankees built
the mansions in Pasadena. By the mid-20th Century there
was La Puente, Monrovia, Rosemead and West Covina
Arteries like Garvey, Valley and Huntington
connected these cities to Azusa.

The San Gabriel watershed begins in the hills above Azusa.
The Angeles National Forest is in the mountains above
San Gabriel. Travelling east from Alhambra to El Monte
to Covina, there are well over a dozen cities in the area code 626
California bungalows and craftsmen cottages dominate
South Pasadena. The protective residents of South Pass
stopped the 710 freeway.

The 10, 210, 710, 60 and 605 are an intricate web of freeways.
Back in the day Route 66 on Foothill Boulevard bisected Azusa.
The Rose Bowl and Rose Parade celebrate the spirit of Pasadena.
Appalachia was replaced by Sriracha in the Valley of San

Gabriel. Boba Milk Tea and dim sum are now iconic in the 626
along with shopping malls and Ikea off the freeway in Covina.

They filmed part of *Back to the Future* in West Covina--
the DeLorean scene in the mall just south of the 60 freeway.
The 57 freeway is a boundary between the 909 and 626.
Duarte and Sierra Madre are neighborhoods west of Azusa.
Spanish colonial revival McMansions and Pho eateries
are in San Gabriel. If you drive north on Rosemead
you'll end up in East Pasadena.

PCC, Art Center and Cal Tech are colleges in Pasadena.
Mt. Sac and Azusa Pacific are colleges east of Covina.
Santa Anita in Arcadia is a landmark north of San Gabriel.
This cluster of locations is rimmed by foothills and freeways.
In' n' Out Burger started in Baldwin Park just west of Azusa.
This huge pocket between LA and the Inland Empire is the 626.

Travel from Pasadena to Pomona on the freeways
or take Arrow Highway from Covina to Azusa.
The Changs live next door to the Diazes
in the San Gabriel Valley and 626.

Unleashed

Unpredictable like January Rain
Santa Ana Winds come from the East
Eucalyptus trees in the left turn lane
Mother Nature unleashed on Pasadena streets

Blind Faith, Sour Grapes & Outside My Window

1.

Saturday started with my tour-guiding shift. I had 24 blind multicultural teenagers walking with me on Hollywood Blvd. The day's challenge involved expanding my standard descriptive capacity. They inspired me to slow down and explain slower, tactile interaction with the landscape became the mandate. They each put their foot in Johnny Depp's footprint. They were bashful like most kids with an extra spark of inquisitiveness.

"Why is the theater called the Chinese?" "Was the owner Chinese?"

"Why is this theater called the Egyptian?" "Is this where the Oscars are?"

Their carefree vigor and joy of life despite their blindness made them great company.

We did a poem south of Hollywood Blvd. They ended up schooling me.

2.

Hours later, Emi, Eka & I are at the Egyptian Movie Palace to watch *Totoro*, Eka's favorite flick. Our seats are among the best in the house, the very back row next to the aisle. Fever is in the air, this is my daughter's first time seeing it on the big screen. She knows all the lines already. We tell her to keep it down, but she's not too loud. Still shortly into the film, a woman directly in front of us turns around, with a hard frown and says,

"If she won't be quiet, take her OUTSIDE!"

This old battered iceberg had a lot of nerve watching a children's film in a theater filled with parents and kids acting so belligerent. Eka kept quiet after this, nonetheless I wanted to curse the woman out. Her nasty field of energy was the polar opposite of the magnanimous blind teenagers. I left it alone but it reminded me that the city is filled with sour souls. The range is infinite in the urban electromagnetic spectrum.

3.

A few nights later, I'm up writing shortly after midnight. I hear distant cries of quarreling lovers. I do my best to ignore it, I've heard it in our neighborhood from time to time. Twenty minutes later, I hear a series of gunshots. Ka-boom! Ka-boom! Ka-boom!! Damn near a dozen shots fired, I hear it all too well. Not sure who was shot. The shooting was close to the house I know that much. I'd heard gunshots before, but this was the closest and the loudest.

My heart rate immediately jumped up as a barrage of different thoughts and what if scenarios raced through my mind. Was it that fighting couple? I thought about my family downstairs asleep. After the sirens and ambulances came I decided to go outside and see what happened. There was a fire-truck and a dozen cop cars on Atlantic.

After a few steps across the street, I remember Emi and Eka are inside asleep. I decide to go back in the house. It was 1AM, I had a writing deadline and nothing but trouble could come from being outside. The next day I learned the police fired the bullets, it was an officer involved shooting; a man was shot by police after he jumped out of the car with a gun in his hand. It turned out to be the same man that was fighting with his girlfriend earlier. The police had been called about a domestic disturbance.

If he had kept his cool he'd still be here today. I heard it all too clear right outside my window.

"Time is time join the masses on the move.
All my artists & activists steady show & prove,
Show & prove with the needle & the groove,
I got the kind of rhymes that'll make your mind move…"

–DJ Dusk aka Tarek Captan

Something in the Water: Hip Hop History in Cerritos

Dating back to the mid-1980s, the City of Cerritos in Southeast L.A. County has played a major role in Southern California Hip Hop history. The geography and demographics of this gateway city have made it a springboard for the mobile DJ culture and a cadre of journalists, writers and artists. This essay will explicate the Hip Hop history and offer a brief portrait of several writers and artists who grew up in Cerritos.

Amid Cerritos's great ethnic diversity, there is also a powerful sense of community. This community can especially be seen in the city's arts and culture. The Beat Junkies and Cerritos All Stars are two of the most well-known DJ crews in Southern California. I have heard many stories from both groups, primarily from DJ Rhettmatic of the Beat Junkies and KJ Butta from the Cerritos All Stars.

They both also pointed out a slew of other artists, writers and musicians who grew up in Cerritos. I will highlight more of these individuals at greater length near the conclusion of this piece. One of these individuals named by KJ Butta is the reporter and broadcast journalist Hetty Chang from NBC 4 in Los Angeles. Chang grew up in Cerritos and attended Whitney High School. She recently spoke at her elementary school, Cerritos Elementary on Career Day.

Before her presentation she shared her insight with me via email on why so much talent has come from Cerritos. She writes:

"From the outside, Cerritos just looks like a nice, well-manicured suburb, but it is so much more than that. There's something in the water in Cerritos—I feel like it breeds success. It has all the ingredients—good schools, people, diversity... community."

Chang is an Emmy-nominated reporter that has made her hometown proud. In a previous article for *KCET* I wrote about the airplane crash that happened in Cerritos in the late 1980s and how I had heard the collision as it crashed into the ground. Chang lived a few doors down from where this crash happened.

After reading my essay, she shared her memories with me in more detail. She writes, "A huge story also influenced my decision to become a reporter when a big news story quite literally landed in my neighborhood. It was in the late 1980's when an AeroMexico DC-9 took a nose dive straight into a row of homes, five houses away from mine. I was struck by the enormity of this tragedy, and drawn to the many heartbreaking stories I watched on the evening news."

"I realized, journalists have an enormous responsibility—to tell people's stories ...accurately and passionately," she says. "To this day, I feel like this job is a privilege, and if I ever feel like it isn't anymore... I'll know I'm not in it for the right reasons. 25 years later I'm working side by side with the very reporters who covered that crash in my neighborhood."

Chang's conviction and sincerity is the same quality that exists in the Hip Hop DJs, writers and artists that came from Cerritos. The first segment of this story begins with the Beat Junkies.

The Beat Junkies

The Filipino community in Cerritos has been very influential in the Southern California Hip Hop scene, especially the mobile DJ crews that emerged from the neighborhood. The mobile DJ crews were known for bringing their turntables, records and speakers to wherever the party was. The parties could be anywhere from a backyard, a warehouse to a wedding reception in a public hall. The Beat Junkies are the most famous of these crews and their rise to prominence is an epic story. The Beat Junkies officially formed in Cerritos in 1992, but their roots started years before.

Nazareth Nirza, better known as DJ Rhettmatic from the world-famous DJ crew, the Beat Junkies grew up in Cerritos. He recently told me his family was, "One of the few first Filipino families that moved to Cerritos. They came to the U.S. in 1968, got situated in Huntington Park (I was born there in 1969), and then moved to Cerritos in 1971." His dad was an engineer and worked for a company called Western Kraft in LA. Western Kraft moved to Cerritos around the same time shortly after his parents moved there. "Their old building is actually on Valley View Blvd, right next to the old Don Juan Mexican Restaurant that used to be there on the corner," he says. "The Beat Junkies used to DJ parties at Don Juan during the early stages before the crew had even manifested."

Rhettmatic notes, "A lot of families from diverse ethnic cultural background moved to Cerritos to start fresh and to pursue the American Dream. Growing up in Cerritos, I had many friends with diverse backgrounds: Whites, Blacks, Latinos, Asians, Christians, Catholics, Muslims, Buddhists, etc.....and growing up around such diversity, you never really thought about the differences, we all just accepted everyone for who they were because it was just the norm."

"I really started to discover Hip Hop when I was in 7th Grade attending Carmenita Junior High," he remembers. "It was one day during lunch time that I saw some of my 8th grade classmates forming a circle near the basketball courts. Somehow, one of the kids brought in a boom-box (Portable Radio/Cassette Tape Player) into school, pulled it out of his duffle bag, and proceeded to press play on the tape deck. What came out of the speakers and what I saw is what changed my whole life."

The music coming out of the boom-box was Afrika Bambaataa and the Soulsonic Force's "Planet Rock." "What was happening in the circle," he says, "was my classmates would start doing these crazy robotic like moves to the rhythm of the music, either dancing with or against each other. This particular dancing was called 'Popping.' I didn't know what it was or the music that was playing, but from that day, I was hooked!"

Rhett describes the spirit of the era, "When Hip Hop first broke out into the West Coast in the early 80's, those were exciting times because it was so fresh, so new, so raw...but we really didn't know how much of an impact it was going to be to us kids, and to the whole world," he says. "Older kids were already listening to Funk groups like Zapp, The Time, Prince, Parliament/Funkadelic. My first cassette tape was Zapp's "Zapp II" and The Time "What Time Is It?" The Sugar Hill Gang's "Rapper's Delight" (the 1st Rap song I've ever heard) was starting to play on radio stations like the Mighty 690 or KIIS FM."

Dating back to the mid-1980s, Cerritos was a hotbed for talent when it came to Hip Hop. "I don't know what was in the water in Cerritos during those days," Rhettmatic says. "A few of our local Poppers and B-Boys (media term: Break-dancers) were featured in the early Hip Hop documentary 'Breakin' & Enterin' and the TV show 'Fame.' Legendary dancer, Shabba Doo (aka "Ozone" from the movie "Breakin") lived in Cerritos at one time. We also had a few local MCs/Rappers that were ahead of their time but never got the recognition they deserved."

"Cerritos had some of the best DJs in the burgeoning Mobile DJ scene," Rhettmatic says. "Early groups like Publique Image and the Ultra Dimensions were throwing local Funk parties at Cerritos College in the late 70's/early 80's that people from the surrounding areas would travel to attend. And get this.... these DJs were Filipino Americans." Rhettmatic grew up watching these guys, especially one named DJ Curse, "Curse was like a big brother/mentor of sorts to me when I was growing up. Even though he was only a year older than me, I would follow him around like an annoying little brother and wanted to be just like him." As the years went on, they shared many stages together worldwide as members of the Beat Junkies.

In addition to DJ Curse, two African American DJs from Cerritos were early influences for Rhett. They were DJ Antron aka Scratchmatic and DJ Arabian Knight. Rhett explains more, "DJ Antron was one of the first DJs to battle in LA and got his reputation for his skills. He was originally named DJ Scratchmatic and later changed his name to DJ Antron when he won the first DJ Battle at the famed 'Radiotron' club, the first LA Hip Hop club.... this is where the basis of my name "Rhettmatic" originated. DJ Arabian Knight was also a highly skilled raw Hip Hop DJ, who was once an original KDAY Mixmasters from the LA's first Hip Hop Radio Station, 1580AM KDAY. He eventually became an MC/Rapper by the name "Psycho" from the group "Insane Poetry" and worked with LA Hip Hop Legends Rodney O & Joe Cooley and recording artist Sir Mix-A-Lot."

Years later Rhett would find inspiration and friendship from a younger DJ, David Mendoza, who was soon to be known as DJ Melo D. They met in 1991 while Rhettmatic was with his comrade, DJ Icy Ice. Rhett says, "I'd heard through the grapevine that there was this young upcoming cat in Cerritos that had amazing skills." Rhett was a few years older from the previous generation in Cerritos and had yet to meet any younger DJ's who could "cut it up" like the guys he looked up to at the time DJ Curse and DJ What. "When I finally met him," Rhett says "and got to see him in action at garage house party, I was shocked that a young cat that I wasn't aware of, can get busy on the turntables like the way we did. Heck, he was sooo good that it made me went back to start practicing more."

Rhett says that Melo is a prodigy. "Everything Melo does is clean, technical, precise, yet funky," he says. "Curse and I have been DJing a little bit longer than Melo, being of course we were older than him, but to me personally, he was and still is incredible and was one of the catalysts (as well as Babu, D-Styles, J.Rocc and Shortkut) to step my game up with the newer styles of DJing coming in." Around this time, the crew began to come together. They had the best of both worlds where they were both inspired by each other and had a lot of fun together.

"When you are surrounded by individuals that are as talented as Melo," Rhett says, "You can't help it but to get better. 'Skills sharpens Skills.' From there, that's when Melo started to meet Curse, then J.Rocc, and so forth. Then from there, J.Rocc put Melo down with the Junkies in 1992 when the crew officially started."

The Beat Junkies were established in 1992 by the great DJ, J. Rocc. The original members included J. Rocc, Curse, Rhettmatic, Melo-D, Icy Ice, Symphony, & What?!, Shortkut, D-Styles, Red-Jay, Havik, and Tommy Gun (who joined in late 1992) were later added. DJ Babu was added in late 1993 and Mr. Choc was added in 1996. Several of the members including Curse, What?!, Rhettmatic, Melo-D and DJ Havik are from Cerritos. Rhett told me more about where the rest were from: "The other Junkies were from other cities: J.Rocc (who formed the Beat Junkies) was from Orange County via Connecticut, D-Styles and Shortkut (they were Beat Junkie members before they've become members of Invisibl Skratch Piklz) are from the Bay Area (Fremont and Daly City), Icy Ice and Symphony are from Carson, Tommy Gun was from

Culver City, Babu is from Camarillo, and Mr. Choc is from Bakersfield."

All and all, they have been one of the most legendary DJ crews for over a generation now. A documentary made by LRG clothing titled *For the Record*, explains more about their history.

Around the same time the Beat Junkies came to rise, Sublime and No Doubt were rocking backyard parties around Long Beach, the South Bay and Northern Orange County. I was at a few of the backyard parties in the early 1990s, but it was really in the clubs and on the radio in the mid to late 1990s that I came to know the Beat Junkies. In 1995, Rhettmatic and the Japanese-American MC Key Kool, were the first Asian-Americans to release a Hip Hop record titled *Kozmonautz*. During this same time, Rhettmatic became a West Coast DMC champion as a solo battle DJ, and won 2 International Turntable Federation World Champion titles with the Beat Junkies. By this time, they were touring internationally.

Years later I met Rhettmatic at Up Above Records in Long Beach along with his fellow members of the Visionaries, Key Kool and LMNO. Rhett has recorded albums with the Beat Junkies, individually and as the DJ for the underground super-group the Visionaries. He's also collaborated with luminaries like J Dilla, Madlib and Talib Kweli among many others. Along with the other members from the Beat Junkies, they have won more awards and produced more records than there's space to mention.

There's much more to say about Rhettmatic and the Beat Junkies, but not enough space here to say it. The only other West Coast mobile DJ group who can match their legacy is the Bay Area crew, the Invisibl Skratch Piklz. Oliver Wang, the Hip Hop journalist and Long Beach State Sociology Professor wrote a book on Duke University Press, *Legions of Boom: Filipino American Mobile DJ Crews in The San Francisco Bay Area*, that offers more on their story and the larger story of mobile DJ crews.

What's especially important to say here though, as Rhettmatic tells me, is that, "Hip Hop helped spawned a generation of Cerritos kids that were truly immersed in the Hip Hop Community whether the public realized it or not including the early 90's Hip Hop group/recording artists Brotherhood Creed, the Crooks N Castles lifestyle brand, the Creative Recreation shoe brand, Ryu from the 90's West Coast independent Hip Hop group, Styles Of Beyond, recording artists Fort Minor associates of Mike Shinoda of Linkin Park, graffiti artists: NASA Crew, and of course, a few individuals from the Beat Junkies."

Rhettmatic says that, even the Mayor of Cerritos, Mark Pulido, was a part of the Hip Hop community. "I grew up with Mark from around the way, we are the same age and we're both Filipino Americans," he says. "He went to Whitney High School, and I went to Cerritos High, and we were from different crews competing against each other. As we got older, we both took different routes in life, but what connected us together and made us become friends to this very day, was Hip Hop."

Rhettmatic is thankful for his crew and his city. In 2015 he told me, "I'm blessed and privileged to be a part of a crew with such caliber of talent. And even more blessed and privileged to still be friends with most of the guys in the crew. We had a lot of ups and downs and went through a lot of trenches/disagreements together, yet the fact that we're still friends and still a crew together after all these years, is a big accomplishment in itself, probably bigger than all the titles and accolades that we've accomplished together or individually."

Kazu Okamoto is a longtime friend of the Junkies from the early days and was from a South Bay DJ crew called "Red Alert." He told me, "They went from DJing house parties, weddings and hall dances to becoming resident club DJs, radio DJs, seasoned battle champions, producers and prominent Hip Hop artists and entrepreneurs. All the while still staying true to what brought them together in the first place - The love of Hip Hop, DJ culture and each other. To top it off, they are still the best DJs on the planet...and it's great to see them being compensated for all the hard work and energy they've put into it throughout the years."

Cerritos All Stars

DJ KJ Butta from the Cerritos All Stars crew grew up watching Rhettmatic and Mayor Mark Pulido. He says, "I met Mark Pulido, when I was 12 years old and interested in dancing with Club Kaibigan, the Filipino club at Whitney High, which he started." KJ Butta attended both Cerritos High School and Whitney High School and graduated in 1992. He was able to buy his first turntables after selling men's shoes at Nordstrom's in the Cerritos Mall. He recalls spending his formative years watching DJ greats like Rhettmatic, Curse and DJ Melo-D.

"My very first junior-high dance was at Room 13/14 at Whitney High School back in 1988. I was super excited to go and dance, but was blown away by the DJ's, Publique Image with Double Platinum," he says. "It was my very first time seeing DJ Rhettmatic and DJ Curse spin and scratch and it was amazing to me."

Originally KJ Butta was into dancing and then he eventually started spinning records his freshmen year in college. He was a year behind another Beat Junkie, DJ Melo-D while he attended Whitney High School. He remembers seeing, "DJ Melo-D wearing his white hooded sweatshirt airbrushed with his name and DJ figure on it. Melo-D used to spin with Modern Muzique and did a lot of dances in the area. I started DJing after high school because I wanted to spin the records I loved to dance to and was exposed to because of Rhettmatic, Curse, Melo-D, etc."

The DJ crew known as the Cerritos All Stars are a few years younger than the Beat Junkies and they are internationally acclaimed as well. They came together in 1995. KJ Butta says, "The Cerritos All Stars is a culmination of 4 different mobile groups: Audio FX Productions, Icon Events (formerly Top Priority), Grand Groove Productions (my crew) and Fascination Productions. We were all asked to DJ a friend's 18th birthday but to bring different equipment. So there was this super group DJing for her and we didn't know what to call ourselves, so I suggested that we would be the Cerritos All Stars." The Cerritos All Stars have followed the model created by the Beat Junkies and have also won their share of awards and toured internationally.

Over the years KJ Butta also worked with the Hip Hop apparel company from Cerritos, Mixwell USA. "My three years at Mixwell helped me solidify my relationships with various DJ's, music lovers, retail and clothing distributors worldwide," he says. "It was through Mixwell that I became friends with and went on tour with The Pharcyde as their road manager back in 2006 and got gigs in Stockholm and opened up for Dilated Peoples and Jurassic 5 in Hawaii."

The Cerritos All Stars have had a popular internet radio show for over a decade and have achieved their own international acclaim like their role models, the Beat Junkies. Like Hetty Chang and Rhettmatic, KJ Butta attributes his success to the diverse landscape of Cerritos. "Growing up in Cerritos helped me understand diversity in community and how to apply that when rocking a party. You're going to have different people that like different things, but if you can blend the different styles in a way that works for everyone, then it makes the party that much better," he says. The fertile cultural landscape of Cerritos has been very good to both the Beat Junkies and Cerritos All Stars.

Elegy to Root Down & Firecracker

"LA loves a good funeral," says DJ J-Logic to me in December 2009 at the final night of the world-famous club known as the Root Down. Hundreds of folks braved a cold Cali night to come one last time to one of the greatest weekly clubs Los Angeles has ever seen. The Root Down and two other clubs, Firecracker and the Chocolate Bar characterized the late 90s Millennial Los Angeles Hip-Hop, funk, soul underground. Sharing a synergy like the Jungle Brothers, A Tribe called Quest and De La Soul, these three Jams exploded with musical energy. Fierce DJ's, live performances, Hip-Hop, rare groove, future soul. People, music, vibes, beats, bass, life. A generation of us can testify, it's been an amazing ride.

A remarkable era ended in December 2009 when Firecracker and Root Down both held their curtain calls a day apart. On December 17, 2009, the "Root Down," held every Thursday for the last 13 years concluded its run. The next day "Firecracker," held twice a month on Friday for the last 12 years had their finale. Closing these two leviathans in the same week, on consecutive days fits because they shared electricity and participants. For those of us coming of age in the 1990's these two Jams are sacred, epitomizing the postmodern metropolis' cosmopolitan funk finesse. Universal, soulful, multicultural, emerging worldwide tribe people. Underground intelligentsia, the Los Angeles avant-garde.

Los Angeles club culture
is burning like a firecracker
People are loving the euphoria…
Sweat is pouring, people bouncing…

Ladies scent lingers on body movement
Nothing matters but the music!

These jams are influential in a way the Sunset Strip or Cahuenga could never be. The jam wasn't just a party, meat market or sloppy bar scene; it was an underground space where West Coast Hip Hop kids gathered to build artistic, intellectual & spiritual consciousness. The zeitgeist of this scene corroborates with KRS ONE in his 2009 book *The Gospel of Hip-Hop*. KRS describes the JAMS held by Kool Herc in the South Bronx around 1973 at the birth of Hip-Hop: "Jams were a creative escape. It was a time to step outside the confinement of mainstream life and create ourselves, to dress up in the clothes ("gear") that amplified what we thought of ourselves, to talk, walk and live according to our perception of ourselves without compromise."

Creative youth coming together to express themselves without compromise begins in the underground. Underground youth created Hip-Hop, Punk rock, and graffiti art. The ethos of underground culture is universal. As KRS ONE writes, "The actual idea of a Jam was to set up a time and a space where the true intentions of our heart could be manifested through our various forms of street recreation, and Kool Herc was the guy that brought everyone together though his deejayin."

The Gangs All Here

The movement that evolved into the Root Down, Firecracker & Chocolate Bar emerged from underground Los Angeles. Backyard jam sessions, the Good Life Café, Acid Jazz, Peace Pipe, Unity, URB Magazine, graffiti crews, East Coast Hip-Hop, b-boy battles, Echo Park art parties. The city's energy after the 1992 Riots created a fertile landscape for music and art. I started UCLA in the fall of 1992 where I met Phillip Martin aka Phillharmonic. We were connoisseurs of music and knowledge, driving all over Los Angeles hitting hip hop shows, house clubs, house parties and a few raves; but it wasn't until Root Down, Firecracker or Chocolate Bar that we were embraced by a community of creative people. Poets, painters, photographers, designers, DJ's, visual artists and educated partiers. We found each other and ourselves on the dance floor. By 1999, we hit the city nightly. We would perform spoken word somewhere earlier and then close down Root Down, Firecracker or Chocolate Bar. A ritual. Sometimes we had girlfriends, other times the boys were rolling. No matter what always golden. Vibing with Rich, Francis, Blackbird, Marcus Gray, Jeremy Sole, Hollywood 7 & Stricke-9. Great friends, great times, great music. KRS One is accurate with his description of jams as a place where kids come to create themselves. We created ourselves every night in the city. Poets, DJ's, emcees, musicians, singer-songwriters, photographers and filmmakers together to the beat of one drum.

Enter the Dragon

Enter the Dragon was a wicked Friday night poetry party from 1999 to 2002 held in a small gallery on the west end of the alley from Firecracker. Punk rock literary, hip-hop academic, a lively reading hosted by poets from the Onyx. We used to slide in the rotation and yell a few poems. After poems at Enter the Dragon, we went next door to Hop Louie. Hop Louie is an old bar just north down the alley from Enter the Dragon. After a few drinks at Hop Louie we'd go back over to Firecracker and keep dancing.

Old school denizens like Musicman Miles Tackett, Loslito, Marvski, Yem, Mear One & Ordell Cordova talk about events from the late Eighties and early Nineties like Radiotron, Water the Bush, Peace Pipe & Brass. Those events were before my time, for me it's been Root Down, Firecracker and Chocolate Bar. Over the years there were several periods where we went almost every time. There were also months where we didn't go as much but we'd always go back.

For years and years, we gathered on every other Friday at Firecracker! Part of the mystery was exactly which Friday was it on. They held it on the 1st, 3rd & 5th Friday of every month so you always had to check the calendar and count Friday's. Then you had to drive to Chinatown and find it. Finding it is confusing because you walk into a long alley between Broadway and Hill Street. Then suddenly it appears: the Quon Brothers "Grand Star Restaurant." Behold a sea of people in a long corridor of Chinese stores and street lamps. The alley in front of Firecracker is magical on its own. Some heads would just stay in the alley all night long. I remember the first time there and the thrill of walking through the Chinatown alleys hearing the distant drums.

Firecracker's home is the Quon Brothers "Grand Star Restaurant," a two-floor Chinese Restaurant on Broadway. Firecracker was founded by a coalition of artists, activists, writers, photographers, filmmakers & DJ's in 1998. Co-founder Lisa Yu says, "When the idea of Firecracker was first conceived, Daryl Chou, myself, James Kang and a few other friends envisioned an artistic space where local writers, poets, visual artists and musicians could come together to perform, share and inspire. We craved a space where our community could come together to create and grow, so we wanted to make sure that this party incorporated not only the music that inspired us, but also other artistic elements that were part of our scene."

They called up four DJ friends of theirs: Wing Ko, Eric Coleman, Alfred Hawkins and Paris Potter to be the original DJ's. Firecracker was born in August of 1998. Before long the location, the people and the music merged into one. Lisa Yu says, "We showcased artists who inspired us... Chaz Bojorquez, Omar Ramirez, Angelo Moore (of Fishbone), Mear One, HVW8 crew etc." Yu continues, "Quickly, and beyond what we ever imagined, our intimate party grew into something much larger. Logic, Azul and Kutmah eventually joined the crew and it took on a life of its own" They also teamed up with like-minded orgs like Giant Robot, Stones Throw Records, Mochilla & Chocolate Bar to cross-pollinate the party.

Filmmaker and photographer Brian Cross aka B+ says, "When Firecracker opened most people didn't even know where Chinatown was - let alone go down there to socialize. Daryl, Alfredo, Lisa Yu, Wing, Jim, C Boogie, Paris and Coleman built an institution on the backs of a bi-weekly party that was simply that. Good music, fun times, cool space. In the process, a whole scene grew up around that part of town and many legends graced the doors of Frank's Grand Star."

I can't even count how many artists I met there over the years. Coleman, B+, AzuL, Frohawk Two Feathers. Many times, the vibe rocked so hard folks would be in the alley till 3AM and still ready for afterhours. Romances, whirlwind relationships, freestyle sessions, young friends, rite of passage. We all grew up together. Friendships formed, bridges got built, connections were made. I met my wife, the mother of my daughter and son at Firecracker.

Daryl Chou, one of the cofounders of Firecracker never missed one over 12 years. He was there every two weeks from August 1998. This dedication is an overlooked factor in longevity. Consistency like Daryl's and resident DJ's like Eric Coleman is the main ingredient needed to create an event with the staying power of Firecracker. Stalwarts like Miles Tackett, Carlos Guaico and DJ DUSK hardly missed a week at Root Down over the same period.

NO SOUND IN TOWN LIKE THE MIGHTY ROOT DOWN!

The Root Down's story is every bit as epic as Firecracker. Founded by Miles Tackett and Carlos "Loslito" Guaico, the Root Down began in 1996 at a Coffeehouse jam session on La Brea. Originally called "The Breaks," Miles organized a group of players to play a set of funk classics and the rest is history. Musicians, b boys, live players, graff writers, all came together. The band BREAKESTRA came from those jam sessions. Over the next three years the event grew larger and moved around.

There was Pedro's on Vermont in Los Feliz, the Atlas Supper Club in Koreatown and Gabah on Melrose & Normandie. Root Down stayed at Gabah for six years before moving to Little Temple in 2004. In 2009, it moved to El Cid. The resident DJ's were many. Beginning with Dusk, Miles Tackett, Loslito, Mixmaster Wolf, Cut Chemist, and Wyatt Case. Others include Egon, Marvski, SloePoke, DJ Jedi, DJ A Ski, Ervin, Charles the Goat & DJ Destroyer. Surprise guests like the Beat Junkies, DJ Shadow, Madlib and countless more talented selectors in the Los Angeles sector rocked the Root Down.

The Root Down's live performances became a springboard for underground hip-hop, funk and soul in Los Angeles. Every week artists like the Breakestra, Jurassic 5, Cut Chemist, Beat Junkies, Dilated Peoples, Darkleaf, People Under the Stairs, Loot Pack, Ugly Duckling, Visionaries, Crown City Rockers, Aloe Blacc, DJ Exile, Procussions and others rocked the stage. The annual Anniversary parties were large. Especially when you had to park your car in Little Tokyo and ride the Funky Bus to the actual location. These jams went till 4AM.

Among the most memorable Root Down's are the Soundclashs. It started from a late-night conversation between DJ Dusk and Miles Tackett. A Soundclash started in Jamaica when rival DJ's would battle one another with their sound systems. They would battle each other to see who had the loudest and largest sound system. Basically, coming down to: Who rocks the hardest?

The crowd would follow the loudest sound system and people dancing would surround the winner of the Soundclash. In New York City, particularly the South Bronx in 1973, DJ Kool

Herc (who was also Jamaican) had the largest sound system in the borough. As KRS One noted above, Herc's famous jams are known as the birthplace of Hip-Hop. Dusk wanted Los Angeles to know this history. Besides being a great DJ, he was a natural Ethnomusicologist. He loved history so deeply that he decided to host a Soundclash in Los Angeles.

The first battle was Madlib versus Cut Chemist in 2001. They battled beat for beat on the Root Down stage. The crowd's ovation determined who rocked the hardest. They battled four rounds. Dusk hosted the battle, egging the crowd on:

"Los Angeles!! If you're feeling alright now, make some motherfu#$in' nooooiiiisse & let me knooooooooow!!"

Cut Chemist had timed voice-overs and a well-crafted routine. Madlib made spontaneous beats relentlessly. The next Soundclash was Will I Am of Black Eyed Peas battling Thes One of People Under the Stairs in 2002. Will I Am & Thes One have ideological differences, check the footage. The third Soundclash featured OHNO of Stonesthrow battling DJ Exile.

Mochilla Productions filmed all three Soundclashs with hand held cameras. Mochilla is the Production Company of well-respected filmmaker/photographer B+ and his comrade, DJ/Filmmaker/photographer Eric Coleman. They've shot over 100 album covers and traveled the world documenting music. Their recording of the Soundclash is a snapshot of West Coast underground Hip-Hop history. The DVD film is *DJ DUSK'S ROOT DOWN SOUNDCLASH.*

The program of all three Soundclash's is continuous. No edits, no overdubs, and no interruptions—just raw Hip-Hop. Coleman told me, "It was like witnessing the West Coast Beat Street or Style Wars only 20 years later." Dusk's effusive energy on screen for two hours is timeless. His persona is pure hip hop,

B-boy existentialism. Mochilla never intended to release this film but when DJ Dusk tragically passed in 2006, they felt it was important to honor his legacy and share his genius. His years of service at the Root Down set a benchmark for DJ excellence.

Records like "Running Away," by Roy Ayers remind me of DJ Dusk & Wyatt Case going back and forth playing funk & soul. For many after Dusk left, Root Down was never the same. Therefore, the Soundclash footage is so vital. After a decade of rocking, a drunk driver killed Dusk in 2006. He was 31 years young. Dusk loved Los Angeles. He inspired Miles Tackett to begin DJing. "I will always remember the times," says Miles, "that Dusk & I would get into one for one record sessions toward the end of the night inspiring & sometimes challenging each other to bring a track that was not the same ol same ol but still rocked the party."

Miles taped a verse by Dusk that appears on the Breakestra's 2009 record. The song "`Posed to Be," was recorded just before Dusk passed. Dusk rhymes with Mixmaster Wolf & J-5 legend Chali 2na. Check his verse:

I'm the time of day when sun & moon meet
When the heaven's shine beautifully & night & day greet:
Dusk! Hey yo, I'm known for nice blends
If ya like the way it feels-notify your friends.
Time is time join the masses on the move.
All my artists & activists steady show & prove,
Show & prove with the needle & the groove,
I got the kind of rhymes that'll make your mind move…

Dusk's verse captures the verisimilitude of the Root Down/ Firecracker movement. Artists, activists, show and prove, the power of people coming together and the gospel of music. Dusk's spirit lives on. The Breakestra titled their Fall 2009 album *DUSK TILL DAWN*. After playing a series of November shows that Fall in Europe, they made it home just in time to play the final Root Down.

WE ARE THE MOVEMENT

On my way to the last Root Down I went by Mochilla's storefront in Glassell Park. They were showing a collection of B+ & Coleman's 14 by 17-inch prints. Close to a hundred fine art photos dating back to the late Eighties hung in a space just over 1200 square feet. The range of images shows how far they've traveled. Shots of David Axelrod, Lalo Schifrin, Saul Williams, DJ Shadow, Madlib, OHNO, the Stonesthrow artists, MF Doom, Invisible Scratch Pickles, NWA, Azymuth. Photos in Brazilian record shops. Landscapes upon landscapes. Neon skylines, decaying houses, New York City, New Orleans, Columbia, London. The pictures tell the story. Mochilla's been cataloging the movement. I ran into Andrew Lojero, Porschia Baker, Rocio Contreras, B+, Coleman and Black Shakespeare.

After I left Mochilla, I drove to Silverlake to get painter Mear One. Mear has painted live at the Root Down many times, including the opening night in 1996. Though neither one of us had gone in a minute, we couldn't miss the last Root Down. We carpooled to El Cid near the Sunset Junction. The lopsided stairs of El Cid slope down 30 feet below Sunset Blvd. Mear One and I spent time in the patio outside with old friends because the dance floor and DJ area were mobbed. We posted with cosmic individuals like Longevity, Marvski, Rosalinda, J-Logic, Adriana, Felicia, Karla, Doll One, Arturo, EarL, Frank E., Vinnie, AzuL, Wyatt Case and DJ Concise. This is when J Logic said, "LA loves a good funeral."

We reminisced like Pete Rock & CL Smooth. Memories like one late night when Dusk dropped into the mix DMX's, "WE RIGHT HERE!" It wasn't that often they played DMX, but the way Dusk mixed the beat in was so smooth that we felt the euphoria DMX must have felt when he yelled, "We're not going anywhere, we right here!!"

For that moment in time, DMX's fiery voice captured the passion and loyalty we had for each other and the music. The crowd danced with fever chanting, "We're not going anywhere, we right here!" Some nights we danced till the lights came on.

Almost two decades ago, entering the new millennium, Chocolate Bar, Root Down and Firecracker set the precedent for the next generation of jams: Sound Lessons, Funky Sole, More, Bounce Rock Skate, Sunday Service, Descarga, Quality, Afro Funke, Soul Sessions, Sketch Book, the Do-Over, the annual Thanksgivends and the Low End Theory. Kindred events like Juju, hosted by the Soul Children, Deep with Marques Wyatt and Nappy at the Roots with Medusa and Lady Copper. Chocolate Bar rocked till 2008. Now Chocolate Bar founders Aurelito and Shakespeare (I'n'I Sound) carry on even stronger with their Ice Cream Truck sound system. Though the doors closed at Root Down and Firecracker, their influence reverberates worldwide continuing at jams like Funky Sole, Soul Sessions, Soul in the Park, Low End Theory, Bridges and Boombox. In the words of DJ Dusk, "We're not done, we're not done!"

Watts to Leimert Park

No matter the conditions, South Central musicians jammed
on the Avenue. Community, Family, Activism, they had to do it.
Music is the heartbeat. The rose that grew from concrete,
surviving restrictive housing covenants, the LAPD, gangs,
the Second World War, nothing could stop the music...

Respect to African-American artists & authors of Los Angeles
from Horace Tapscott to the Watts Writers Workshop,
103rd Street to Leimert Park, Billy Higgins to John Outerbridge.
The spirit of community, Pan Afrikan People's Arkestra,
Ojenke, Quincy Troupe, Kamau Daaood, Watts Prophets,
A.K. Toney, K Curtis Lyle, Eric Priestley, Jayne Cortez, Lula
Washington.
Generations of poets, Generations of musicians.

Khoran Harrison, Michael Datcher, Peter J. Harris, the language
of saxophones plays at the World Stage,
the Union of God's musicians.
Underground musicians, hear the Universal order
of black expression
Listen. Listen. Listen.

Back in the day an archipelago of afterhours jam sessions
stretched up and down Central Avenue from Pico to Slauson,
the sound of Los Angeles, Central Avenue, Western, Watts,
Crenshaw—they used to call it all South Central, community
artists, passing the magic.
Generation of poets, generations of musicians.

The media paints a portrait of South Central that overlooks
the people, real people, not some exaggerated mythical evil.

The mythical South Central is used by record and industry executives to sell a gangsta fantasy when most of South Central is about Family, Family...

The artists of South Central are healers promoting Unity... Unity... Chester Himes was ahead of his time he kicked wicked insight about the black man's mind. Italian immigrant Simon Rodia worked after work for three decades on the Watts Towers, bottle caps, glass mosaics, tile work, the three towers are a ship, a half a block west of the Charles Mingus Music Center.

Respect out to Watts finest, Don Cherry, Mingus, Eric Dolphy, Big Jay McNeely, Lester Young, South Central sound champions, Roy Ayers, David Axelrod, Lou Rawls, Ornette Coleman, Merilene Murphy, Ruth Forman, Jenoyne Adams, Imani Tolliver, Shonda Buchanan, Pam Ward, Clora Bryant S. Pearl Sharp, Blackbird, Darkleaf, Jackie Robinson, Nat King Cole, Wanda Coleman, Mixmaster Wolf, Wattstax, Isaac Hayes, Jesse Jackson and people chanting:

> I Am Somebody! I am Somebody!
> You are somebody! We are somebody!
> South Central Los Angeles talk to me...

Living legends like Leon Mobley, Esso Won Books and Ramses, Community is family, Craftsman cottages in West Adams, Jefferson Park, Angeles Vista. Twilight on Slauson, West is west of Crenshaw, Chesterfield Square, Canterbury Knolls, Morningside Circle, Athens on a Hill, South of South Central, South Los Angeles, City of Angels. Music is the heartbeat.

Pan Afrikans Peoples Ark playing South Park now they call it the Barry White Recreation Center. They make magic there. Horace Tapscott passed the magic like Samuel Browne taught him at Jefferson High School. Knowledge is shared, Watts Learning Center, Ralph Bunche, Bunchy Carter, Flo Jo,

Biddy Mason, Walter Mosley, Donald Bakeer, Monster Kody,
Charles Wright and the Watts 103rd Street Rhythm Band.
Express yourself, the world listens... Listens.

Fathers of funk, Poetry pioneers, you gave a voice to the voiceless
Watts Writers Workshop to the World Stage, 5th Street Dicks,
Babe & Rickey's Inn, Project Blowed, Freestyle Fellowship,
Park Bench People, Mikah 9 and Ben Caldwell...

Emissaries called upon to heal Los Angeles children of Chaos.
In the days of Pentecost artists of Watts and Leimert Park celebrate
community, celebrate family, generations of sounds, generations
of voices. You gave a voice to the voiceless.
Generations of poets, generations of musicians.
Branches of a dark tree, the chorus of community tells the story
in paintings, poetry and Black Music. The giant is awakened,
RESPECT TO THE GIANTS of South Central Los Angeles
You are Kings of expression! Music is the Heartbeat...

The History of South Central Los Angeles: A Life or Death Situation

"We are not against development, we're against luxury development," exclaims Donna Liseth Quintanilla. 19-year-old Quintanilla is a co-founder of the South Central Dreamers, a collective of youth activists from South Central Los Angeles who use the arts and activism to fight against gentrification displacement and the school to prison pipeline. Wiser than their years, the South Central Dreamers are a part of a larger multicultural cadre of organizations and activists that are skillfully fighting gentrification and the imminent transformation of South Central Los Angeles.

The combination of rising property values, the lack of rent control, dozens of new condo developments and other forces like Metro Expansion and the relocation of the Los Angeles Rams in nearby Inglewood are all a part of larger process that have made South Central Los Angeles one of the key sites of struggle in Southern California's battle with gentrification. Furthermore, the historically African-American neighborhood, has become increasingly Latino over the last four decades. As famous as South Central is from films, music and popular culture over the last half century, most Angelenos and others around the world do not truly comprehend the historic legacy of the area and how important it is in the larger story of Los Angeles.

"We know much more, it seems, about ancient cities and dead civilizations—the chalices the elders drank from or the raiments warriors wore—than we do about day-to-day life in 'South Central Los Angeles,' beyond the term, beyond the trope," wrote Los Angeles native journalist Lynell George in 2006 for the *Los Angeles Times Magazine*.

This is a favorite quote of Los Angeles County Urban Planner Jonathan P. Bell. Bell has worked the last dozen years in South Central as an embedded urban planner intent on fighting gentrification. Bell is constantly out in the field working with residents and stakeholders. "As a South Central planner," Bell recently said, "I'm doing my part to support the anti-gentrification resistance. I make connections among advocates and bring people together. I help advocates interpret dense municipal ordinances and land use policies." Bell empowers citizens by offering any material, intellectual or infrastructural support they need. Before spotlighting some of the current battles, it is important to discuss South Central's geography and history to show how it got here.

The Birth of South Central

The roots of South Central Los Angeles trace back to the beginning of the 20th Century. The neighborhood that is now known as "Historic South Central," includes the area between the Harbor Freeway on the west, Central Avenue on the east, Washington Boulevard on the north and Vernon Avenue on the south. Though this pocket is about 40 square miles, the name South Central became a larger umbrella turn for Black Los Angeles, a much larger area, stretching all the way to Watts and Compton on the south and west across the 110 freeway into Inglewood and the Crenshaw District. Technically the term South Central was only geographically accurate for the rectangular parcel of the Central Avenue corridor, but as history has shown, neighborhood names in popular culture are not always historically or geographically accurate. A similar misnomer applies to Boyle Heights and pockets of East Los Angeles like Maravilla, Belvedere and City Terrace.

Historian Steve Isoardi writes about how the term South Central came to rise in his book *The Dark Tree*. "Lured by an expanding economy and the prospect of jobs, the relatively low cost of real estate, a mild climate, and a seemingly less-overt racism," Isoardi states, "African Americans began moving to Los Angeles in large numbers after 1900. For the next forty years their numbers doubled every decade and by 1940 represented slightly more than 4 percent of the total population."

Right from the beginning of this period, the city was already segregated because of racially restrictive housing covenants written into the property deeds. These covenants were not only enforced through the property deeds; the banks and insurance companies also indirectly enforced them through the practice of denying loans, insurance policies and other financial services for African Americans that attempted to sidestep their enforcement. This practice is better known as "Redlining," and it continued well after the covenants were declared unconstitutional in 1948.

One of the only areas not covered in these restrictive covenants extended south from Downtown Los Angeles along Central Avenue all the way to Slauson. As Isoardi states, "By 1940, approximately 70 percent of the black population of Los Angeles was confined to the Central Avenue corridor and relied upon the Avenue to meet all of its social needs." Because this stretch was along the southern section of Central Avenue, the term "South Central Los Angeles," gradually entered the local vernacular by the 1920s. As noted above, "South Central," became a blanket term for all of Black Los Angeles from Central Avenue to Watts to the Crenshaw District.

The African American population doubled because of the Second World War. The need for workers in the aerospace industry and other wartime jobs caused the United States Government to make it illegal for government contractors to discriminate in hiring. The opening of these jobs lured thousands of African Americans to Los Angeles in the 1940s.

Lonnie G. Bunch, a longtime historian with the Smithsonian Institute writes, "Between 1942-1945, some 340,000 Blacks settled in California, 200,000 of whom migrated to Los Angeles." Nonetheless because of the restrictive covenants there were very few places they could move to.

As Professor Paul Robinson writes, "In the wake of Executive Order 8802, hundreds of thousands of blacks migrated to Los Angeles to work in the newly opened defense industries. Subsequent overcrowding in Los Angeles 'Black Belts' caused the housing crisis to become the number-one issue facing Los Angeles's black community during this time." Bunch explains further that, "The greater the Black population grew, the more tightly enforced were the restrictive housing covenants. Though the Black community doubled in the 1940s, it remained confined to pre-war boundaries."

The Great Migration

This period is known as "the Great Migration." It was also the heyday of Central Avenue as a Jazz District and the West Coast Harlem. Numerous eateries, music venues and nightclubs like the Lincoln Theater and Club Alabam stretched from Pico to Slauson from the 1920s to early 1960s. The Dunbar Hotel at 42nd Place and Central was where jazz luminaries like Billie Holiday, Duke Ellington, Ella Fitzgerald and Lester Young would stay when they visited Los Angeles. Hollywood's biggest celebrities like Marilyn Monroe, Rita Hayworth and Orson Welles would regularly visit the Avenue and so did the notorious mobster Mickey Cohen. Despite the storied musical and cultural history, the lack of housing and overcrowding made for poor living conditions.

In 1948, the court case "Shelley v. Kraemer" rendered the restrictive housing covenants illegal. Gradually through the 1950s, the southern section of Los Angeles, from Watts and west towards Inglewood and the Crenshaw District, became increasingly African American. Moreover, during this era, West Adams, Leimert Park and Baldwin Hills gradually became middle class and upper middle-class African American areas. Perhaps no writer has chronicled South Central as much as the Watts-born poet, journalist and screenwriter Wanda Coleman. Born in 1946, during the height of the Great Migration, Coleman documented the area in hundreds of poems and essays written from the mid-1960s to her untimely demise in November 2013.

In an extended essay from 2005 titled "Dancer on a Blade," Coleman ruminates on her South Central childhood. "I grew up in the South Central of the Fabulous '50s," Coleman writes, "which was in relentless flux as a steadily increasing Black population demanded more access to financial, health, and recreational facilities and an end to housing along racial lines."

Coleman remembers that her family was the first Black family on their street. Coleman attended Gompers Junior High and graduated from Fremont High School in 1964. She celebrates the archipelago of "Black Los Angeles," made up of Fremont, Jefferson, Jordan and Washington High Schools. As the 60s went on, Crenshaw, Dorsey and Manual Arts High Schools were also included in this.

Professor Josh Sides has closely documented the last century of Black Los Angeles over the last two decades. His accounts corroborate with Coleman's pertaining to the rising social status of African Americans in the city in the midcentury. As the 1950s gave way to the early 1960s, neighborhoods were desegregated and several of the leading Black churches were beginning to wield political influence in civic affairs. "By the early 1960s," Sides states, "African Americans had significantly transformed their status in Los Angeles. Their protests were widespread, their demands were well known, and their political influence—if still uneven—was undeniable. Most important,

African Americans participated in daily urban life in ways that would have been impossible two decades earlier."

Chief Parker and Interstate 10

Nonetheless though, Sides also notes that "Few issues troubled African Americans in postwar Los Angeles more than the complete deterioration of their relationship with the Los Angeles Police Department." The reputation of the LAPD became especially notorious under the reign of Chief William Parker from 1950 to 1966. Parker is infamous for many reasons. He is credited for not only promoting racial profiling and aggressive policing, but also with harassing businesses and patrons along Central Avenue so frequently that his policing methods led to not only breaking up Central Avenue's vibrancy but the 1965 Watts Riots.

One illustration of Parker's totalitarian tactics is cataloged by Mike Davis in *City of Quartz*. "Under Parker—a puritanical crusader against 'race mixing'—nightclubs and juke joints were raided and shuttered," writes Davis. "In 1954 John Dolphin, owner of Los Angeles's premier R&B record store near the corner of Vernon and Central, organized a protest of 150 Black business people against an ongoing 'campaign of intimidation and terror' directed at interracial trade. According to Dolphin, Newton Division police had gone so far as to blockade his store, turning away all white customers and warning them that 'it was too dangerous to hang around Black neighborhoods.'" It was episodes like this that culminated into the 1965 Watts Riots.

Another issue that stifled the spirit of the community was the California State Highway Commission's campaign to build both the 110 and I-10 through the heart of South Central Los Angeles. The path for Interstate 10 was especially troubling because it cut a 500-foot-wide section through a section of West Adams also known as "Sugar Hill." "Sugar Hill," was considered one of the most beautifully well-kept neighborhoods of African Americans anywhere in America. Josh Sides explains further that, "Believing that the selection of this route was at best insensitive and at worst racially motivated, a group of West Adams residents immediately formed the Adams-Washington Committee, choosing several delegates to present the community's grievances to the commission in Sacramento."

Sides also notes that African Americans in Santa Monica opposed the proposed route through their area too because it bisected the small black community in Santa Monica similarly in the enclave near Pico Boulevard around 26th Street. The great Los Angeles African American poet Kamau Daaood was born in this section of Santa Monica in 1950.

Ultimately, Interstate 10 was built through both neighborhoods destroying hundreds of houses. A similar process happened 10 miles east of Sugar Hill in Boyle Heights where five freeways intersect including the 10. This destructive process of freeway construction through neighborhoods of color not only occurred in Los Angeles, but in Minnesota, the Bay Area, Maryland, Louisiana, Washington, Texas, New York and Massachusetts among other sites. Accounts of the devastation of freeway construction in neighborhoods of color across Los Angeles can be read in both Eric Avila's *The Folklore of the Freeway,* and Helena Maria Viramontes's *Their Dogs Came With Them.* Eric Avila's 2014 book mentioned above spotlights the creative strategies urban communities across America used during the 1950s, 60s and 70s to document and protest the damage highway construction wielded on countless neighborhoods.

"The spate of racial violence that erupted in American cities in the mid-1960s," Avila declares, "shocked white Americans who had insulated themselves within exclusive suburban enclaves, willfully ignorant of inner-city conditions of racial poverty. After riots in the Los Angeles neighborhood of Watts, 1965 became America's

1848, sparking more stringent demands for racial equality and drawing the world's attention to America's latest race problem. In the depths of inner-city despair, highway construction added insult to injury, fanning the flames of racial unrest."

The 1965 Watts Riots and Civil Rights Movement

As Avila insinuates above, issues like highway construction combined with frustration with the LAPD, the brewing unrest of racial inequality and inner-city poverty contributed to the outbreak of six days of rioting in Watts in August 1965. The catalyst for the riots occurred on August 11th on an extremely warm night when a highway patrol motorcycle officer pulled over a young African American man named Marquette Frye for speeding.

A large crowd assembled around the officers as they attempted to arrest Frye and the unrest began from this. Further details on this episode have been written about in countless books, but as Martin Schiesl writes, the six days of rioting "covered about 46 square miles and left thirty-four persons, mostly black dead, 1,032 wounded, and 3,952 arrested. Property damage amounted to $40 million, with over 600 buildings damaged and destroyed." Over the next few years, several similar riots occurred across America, like the 1967 Detroit Riots. These episodes further galvanized the emerging Civil Rights Movement and connected with the creative branch of the Black Power movement, the Black Arts Movement.

Following the long hot summer of 1965, Watts and South Central Los Angeles became a hotbed of the Civil Rights Movement. Organizations like the Studio Watts Workshop, the Watts Writers Workshop, the Watts Tower Arts Center, Pan Afrikan People's Arkestra, the Black Panthers and US Organization utilized both the arts and direct action as methods to raise awareness and attempt to create social change. These groups and many others were highly active in the community well into the mid-1970s. The 1973 documentary film *Wattstax*, captures the magic and optimism of this period. 103rd Street in Watts was one of the epicenters. During this period, the lively artistic and musical spirit that was originally on Central Avenue started moving west to streets like Normandie and Western and eventually to Crenshaw and Leimert Park.

From about 1965 to 1975, the Black Arts Movement in Los Angeles flourished in Southern California. It continued beyond 1975, but economic conditions and public policy in the late 1970s and the rise of Reagan in the 1980s, led to less funding for the arts and more difficult circumstances for artists and musicians to survive. Economic restructuring in the manufacturing sector and other changes in the economy made jobs scarce.

Josh Sides explains that "the mid-1980s represented the nadir of South Central's already tumultuous history. Fueled primarily by the wave of plant closures, black unemployment and poverty rates rose throughout the decade. An analysis of income distribution in black Los Angeles between 1970 and 1990 revealed the polarizing effects of the decline in low-skilled and semiskilled employment among blacks." These conditions also contributed to the rise of the Crack Cocaine economy. Crack offered a quick fix with a high profit margin. Crack was introduced on the South Central streets in the early 1980s and caught on quickly.

The devastation of crack and the rise of gangs across South Central Los Angeles is by now, old news. For many voyeurs around the world, the film and musical depictions of this stereotype became their image of South Central Los Angeles. Even though much of the greater South Central area is well kept small single-family homes, much of the world at large still associate it with films like *Boyz 'n' Hood*, and musical groups like NWA. The Uprisings of 1992 further exacerbated these preconceived notions and the stereotypes only became more prevalent as the 1990s went on.

Simultaneously as the world at large saw South Central one way, the area was transforming demographically.

The Rebirth of South Central

Beginning in the 1980s, South Central started becoming more Latino. Josh Sides writes that during the 1980s, "the Latino population of South Central increased by approximately seventy-eight thousand, whereas the black population decreased by almost seventy thousand. Remarkably, the census of 2000 revealed that the Latino population of South Central (58 percent) finally outnumbered the black population (40 percent)." A variety of factors contributed to this. A sizeable percentage of African Americans sold their homes and moved to the Inland Empire and other locations like Palmdale, Lancaster and even Las Vegas for larger, less expensive and newer houses and better employment opportunities.

Writer Dana Johnson discusses African American families moving to the Inland Empire in her recent book of short stories, *In the Not Quite Dark.* In addition to black families leaving South Central, the emerging Latinization of South Central was not only incoming Mexican residents, but also included Salvadorans. Guatemalans, Nicaraguans, Belizeans and others from Central and South American moving into the area.

This more diverse demographic mix made the Rodney King Uprisings of 1992 even more complicated than 1965. Many of the same frustrations from 1965 remained, but the 1992 version involved more multicultural citizens and a much larger geographic area. Many historians have called 1992's events in Los Angeles, "a postmodern bread riot."

Similar to following 1965, many efforts were made following 1992 to rebuild South Central. There were some new projects, but perhaps one of the best-known changes happened to the name "South Central," itself. In 2003, the city of Los Angeles unanimously voted to change the name South Central to South Los Angeles. This effort was aided by the rise of other smaller micro-neighborhood names like Chesterfield Square, Canterbury Knolls, Athens on a Hill, Green Meadows and Vermont Square among others. There are also areas of Unincorporated Los Angeles County in the vicinity like Florence-Firestone, Athens-Westmont and Willowbrook.

Specific districts within the greater South Central area like Angeles Mesa, Leimert Park, the Crenshaw District and Watts had always existed, but the renaming of South Central to South Los Angeles inspired these other smaller enclaves within the greater area to rebrand themselves with more specific names. Opinions on these changes vary across the board, but some older citizens were happy to discard the South Central name because of the negative connotations that many had associated with it. Other changes that have altered the community's character include the rise of charter schools. There are now dozens of more schools and many of them did not even exist 15 years ago.

Contemporary Community Organizers

All this history brings South Central Los Angeles to this current juncture of gentrification and displacement. As USC continues to expand north and south on Figueroa, Metro expands across the Crenshaw District into Inglewood and the Los Angeles Rams return to town and begin building their new stadium in Inglewood, the greater South Central Los Angeles area is being faced with new issues that further complicate the long-standing ones. Many different organizations in the area are working hard to stop gentrification and displacement, Community Coalition is one of the most established. There is also Strategic Actions for a Just Economy (SAJE) and United Neighbors in

Defense Against Displacement. Each of these organizations are coalitions that include black and brown residents who are united to improve their community and counteract the forces of gentrification. SAJE is where the young activist Donna Liseth Quintanilla of the South Central Dreamers first interned three years ago while still in high school. This experience changed her life and politicized her when she was 17.

Quintanilla attended Jefferson High School and West Adams High School and she has an incredible command of the public policy issues currently facing South Central. I met with her briefly along Central Avenue one late September afternoon and she spoke eloquently about many key issues facing the area like the remodeling of Rolland Curtis, the renovation of Jordan Downs, the new soccer stadium being built at Exposition Park and the lack of affordable housing across South Central Los Angeles. Quintanilla's vocabulary is far beyond her years quoting terms like the AMI, (Area Median Income). Currently attending Trade Tech, she wants to transfer to UCLA to become an Environmental Justice Major and then get her Masters at UCLA in Urban Planning. The Guatemalan-American Quintanilla also works closely with LA County Urban Planner Jonathan Bell.

Bell met Quintanilla through the extended South Central L.A. network during the early days of the vigorous community-driven protest against The Reef. The Reef is a redevelopment project on Washington and Hill that many long-term South Central residents oppose. Bell says, "Donna was out on the front lines pushing back--hard! She was equally active on social media raising awareness about the looming threat of gentrification in South Central. Fearless, undaunted and only 19, Donna is a true resistance leader against South Central gentri-hipsterfication. And she represents the Latina youth leadership at the heart of today's social justice movements." There are many other young activists like Quintanilla.

49-year-old Skira Martinez is the owner and founder of Cielo Gallery on Maple near 32nd Street in the heart of Historic South Central. Martinez is a close cohort of Quintanilla and she will never call South Central, "South Los Angeles." She feels the new name erases the history. There are many others who agree with her. Martinez works closely with three generations of activists from 17 to 77.

Martinez has her finger on the pulse of what's happening in the neighborhood. She believes in living a lifestyle that supports her neighbors. She spends her money in the community, supporting yard sales, thrift stores, street vendors and small family businesses. Furthermore, she has opened her gallery/living space as a site where the immediate community "uses Cielo in very practical ways and in the ways that they choose to rather than me creating and offering programs, workshops etc. that I feel they need or want. The community has created space within Cielo to organize, come together in celebration and to make use of the resources within Cielo for homework projects or to simply store a vehicle or vending equipment in the parking lot. Cielo tends to be whatever it needs to be both to the immediate community and to surrounding communities."

Martinez has worked closely with other local activists like not only the South Central Dreamers but the LA Tenants Union, the Solidarity House of the South on Central Avenue and groups like the Youth Justice Coalition, SAJE and the Community Coalition. She tells me that, "It is the autonomous movements/collectives and community members that are doing the most profound and important work in my community—they are the community—and put people over profit. Collectives like Solidarity House of the South are community based/led and are pushing against gentrification in a way that includes education, healing and keeping cultural practices alive. They understand that the fight against gentrification is directly tied to a history of stolen land and resources. Dreamers of South Central have been very active and present in direct actions against gentrification and in gathering and sharing important information."

"The LA Tenants Union has started a local chapter in South Central and this is great as their mission is to strengthen tenants political power through education and advocacy amongst tenants themselves," Martinez says. "It is us – the community itself – that must and can make the difference by resisting, refusing to negotiate and be pacified into believing that the gentrification of our community the white art spaces, the 'nice new white neighbors' and eventual take over by corporate interests and those they serve will benefit them."

"South Central is being surrounded and swallowed up by USC," she says. She has similar concerns about, "the Metro and plans for the Olympics because they are all including a massive collaboration of corporate interests." Martinez believes in putting people over profit. Well versed in the area's history, she understands the economic and cultural patterns that have shaped Los Angeles. "Communities of color have never been able to choose where we live," she declares, "and wherever we do live and create community, we have always lived under the threat of displacement."

As the beginning of this article states, Martinez and Quintanilla are not against development, they are just against luxury development that displaces and leaves out the residents who have always been in South Central. The history shows how displacement has already fractured the community, it is because of this why they fight so hard. South Central Los Angeles has always been one of the most important communities in Los Angeles and it always will be. As Skira Martinez says, "The history of South Central says and shows it all and as a community we have no choice but to actively resist by the many means necessary and available. For many, to say that this is life or death is not an exaggeration."

Everyday Heroes of Florence-Firestone

Located directly north of Watts, Florence-Firestone in unincorporated Los Angeles County is one of the most historic neighborhoods in Southern California. This essay spotlights the history of Florence-Firestone and a cadre of its residents and stakeholders who are working tirelessly to improve the community that they love so much.

The history of the area starts in the late 19th Century when the Southern Pacific and Pacific Electric railroads had stops along Florence and Graham streets. The district was originally called Florence-Graham, and it has always had a high density of housing because of the adjacent manufacturing core. In later years, the County rebranded it Florence-Firestone in reference to Florence Avenue and Firestone Boulevard, the 2 major east-west thoroughfares that bisect the community.

Located six miles south of Downtown Los Angeles, the neighborhood is 3.5 square miles and is surrounded by Huntington Park, South Gate and Los Angeles. It is often lumped in with South Central Los Angeles, but it is unincorporated Los Angeles County and not officially part of the City of Los Angeles, though it is directly north of Watts, which is an official city district. The boundaries zig zag a bit, but generally speaking the northern border is Slauson, the eastern border is Alameda, the western border is Central Avenue, and the southern boundary is Century and the neighborhood of Watts. Within the district is an eclectic mix of commercial, residential and industrial zoning. This can especially be seen on streets like Compton Avenue, where storefront churches are next door to small houses, family-run retail stores, and archaic industrial buildings.

Jonathan P. Bell is a Los Angeles County Urban Planner that has been very active in the Florence-Firestone community over the last decade. He tells me, "Up until now, there has been no published history of the Florence-Firestone area, but historians have written about everything else around it." Bell is correct with his assertion—there has been plenty of history recorded about Watts, the Central Avenue Corridor, Huntington Park, and South Gate, all located nearby. Bell is deeply committed to improve Florence-Firestone and to share its untold story. He has worked closely with local residents and the county library to do this. The Boyle Heights-born, Montebello-raised Bell loves South Los Angeles as a whole, and takes his job very seriously as urban planner. He knows the area better than just about anyone.

Another fascinating point about the district, Bell tells me, is its zip codes. "California's zip codes run the ninety-thousands," he says. "Florence-Firestone's zip codes are 90001 and 90002. Origination points. The statewide zip codes BEGIN in Florence-Firestone. We cannot deny that history! Yet somehow historians have overlooked the Florence-Firestone community."

The population of Florence-Firestone has always been diverse, dating back to over a century ago. First, it was European settlers in the late 19th and early 20th Centuries, and then African Americans came in the early 20th Century, particularly because of the area's proximity to Central Avenue and Watts. Mexican immigrants soon joined the black population, and by the late 20th Century Latinos from Central and South America started arriving. Florence-Firestone has always served as an origination point for new arrivals to Southern California.

The massive Goodyear Tire and Rubber Company factory, formerly located on Central between Gage and Florence, was a key factor in the area's growing population during the early 20th Century. In its heyday over 2,500 employees worked there and operations ran 24 hours a day, seven days a week for many years. Goodyear even built a small residential tract for its employees early on. A portion of the area was dubbed the Wingfoot Industrial District, in honor of the Goodyear logo. The former Goodyear site is now operated by the United States Postal Service. It is a giant parcel of land that at one point in time even had enough space for a hangar for the earliest versions of the Goodyear Blimp.

Less than two miles southeast of the former Goodyear plant at Alameda and Firestone is the equally massive former plant for Firestone tires. Located in South Gate, this plant was located adjacent to Alameda during the days when the street was like a Berlin Wall in relationship to the restrictive housing covenants in place in Southern California from the early 20th Century. East of Alameda, into areas like South Gate and Huntington Park, were white neighborhoods considered off limits to people of color for much of the 20th Century until these covenants were declared unconstitutional in 1948.

Firestone Boulevard's name changes to Manchester a mile west of the former Firestone plant at Central Avenue when it enters the city of Los Angeles. These two large industrial hubs were not the only industrial sites in the area; there were dozens of other assembly plants and factories within a few mile radius. To this day, there are numerous auto dismantling shops and other small industrial sites on Alameda heading south into Watts.

The housing stock in Florence–Firestone has always been dense, and includes lots of bungalows, duplexes, triplexes, and occasional ranch houses and Victorians to accommodate the working man. Though many of the first residents were working-class whites, often from the South, there were many European immigrants and by the time of the Second World War, large numbers of African-Americans called the area home.

The story of the neighborhood's eventual decline is by now a familiar story that applies to not only South Los Angeles, but also to nearby cities like South Gate, Huntington Park, and other parts of the former manufacturing core, like Lynwood and Compton. The slow decline began with the closing of many of the local factories during the 1960s and '70s, and the slow disinvestment of the area following both the 1965 Watts Uprisings and the 1992 Rodney King Uprisings.

What's less known though, is that crime has gone down dramatically in Florence-Firestone over the last decade. The neighborhood has been making a quiet resurgence in recent years. The improvements can be directly attributed to a few groups of local residents, stakeholders, and county officials that have been working together. For this reason the County of Los Angeles Public Library, in partnership with the Florence-Firestone Community Leaders organization and the Florence-Firestone/Walnut Park Chamber of Commerce, have banded together to create a community history website, called "Florence-Firestone: Stories of Everyday Heroes," that gathers videos, photos and narratives of these "everyday heroes," from Florence-Firestone. This site was the brainchild of Angel Nicolas, a longtime Los Angeles County Public librarian that slowly came to know the Florence-Firestone community and was very impressed with the activists he met. Nicolas has been working very hard over the last year collecting their stories.

On June 24th, 2015 at the Florence-Firestone Service Center, a launch event was held for the website, and several of the community leaders were on hand to share their testimonies. The event was a spirited occasion with a palpable excitement in the air. The Service Center, located on Compton Avenue directly across the street from the historic first Sheriff's Station, was the perfect site to hold this gathering. In its lobby is a large mural, painted in 2010 by the late great South Los Angeles artist Willie Middlebrook, called "Short Stories," depicting the ethnic diversity of the past and present of Florence-Firestone. Middlebrook died in 2012 and this piece was one of his final works. He was well known for loving Los Angeles and doing his best to capture untold stories. He would have been very happy to hear about the "Everyday Heroes" project.

The newly launched site now features video interviews with eight individuals deeply engaged in improving the Florence-Firestone community. Their commitment to improve their neighborhood was truly inspiring. I attended the launch event, and spoke with a number of these leaders. Here are a few of their stories:

William Allen is a Vietnam veteran that grew up in Florence-Firestone during the 1950s, and ended up moving back to the neighborhood 40 years later after retiring from the military. When he moved back into the property his parents had owned, he was disappointed by how decrepit their old home, and the whole area, had become. His parents had rented out their property for many years, and in the course of his travels he had lost touch with his early stomping grounds.

In his video interview, he spoke about how his best friend while growing up was a Mexican-American and that during his day, black and brown residents got along very well. When he returned to the neighborhood, there was more tension than he remembered. Shortly after he moved back into the house his parents had bought in 1954, there was a drive-by shooting next door, and then his home was robbed.

These events led him to visit the local Sheriff's station at Compton Avenue and Nadeau Street, and he was told about the Florence-Firestone Community Leaders organization. He's been a key member of the group from this day on. He now mentors young basketball players, and he remains a leader in the community. At the launch event for "Everyday Heroes," Allen briefly spoke before the crowd about his participation in the group and his deep love for Florence-Firestone.

Another local leader featured on the website and present at the launch is Paula Trejo. Trejo is the President of the Florence-Firestone Community Leaders, and like William Allen she also grew up in the neighborhood and then moved out, only to move back again years later. When she returned in 2004, she was inspired to join up with other local activists like William Allen. She has raised children in the area and is very committed to getting local citizens more services in their community.

Rick Aldridge is also featured on the website and is very active with the Florence-Firestone Community Leaders. He grew up in a politically active family in the area, attending Fremont High School and then went on to both UCLA and Cal State L.A. for his graduate studies. He has been involved in economic development for many years and ended up moving back to the area when his parents were getting older. Like Allen and Trejo, he had been away from the area for many years and when he returned, he decided to contribute to making it better. He now brings his many years of experience in the business world to help the local economy, as well as improve the schools, in Florence-Firestone.

The Florence-Firestone Community Leaders is a diverse group of residents from the area that includes homeowners, business leaders, and working-class residents. They meet every second Wednesday of the month at Washington Park at 6:30 p.m. Above all, they are about community empowerment. Aldridge notes in his interview that they all get along very well and he hopes to transfer this camaraderie across the district. The area was once predominantly black, then by the early '90s, it was equally black and Latino; now it is over 85% percent Latino and about 15% black.

Oral history from Jonathan P. Bell is also featured on "Everyday Heroes," and he works closely with the County Library, the Florence-Firestone Community Leaders, and the Chamber of Commerce. Bell tells me, "Florence-Firestone is one of the best examples of a local community where different groups work together and peacefully coexist." Bell brings his knowledge of zoning codes and local history to the table and anything else they may need. Above all, he loves Florence-Firestone and wants to see the district flourish.

Another local stakeholder featured on the website and present at the launch event is Gloria Medina, the president of the Florence-Firestone Merchants Association. Medina is a strong advocate for women entrepreneurs and has done a lot to stimulate local business. She was awarded two certificates from the County at the event for her service to the community.

One local resident who was at the event is 87-year-old Joseph Jacob Titus, who is yet to be filmed for the website, but will be in the future. Titus is a Caucasian man that has lived his entire life in Florence-Firestone. His father was a contractor that built apartment houses on 59th, 62nd, 63rd, and 64th Street during the 1920s. Titus told me that though his father had been quite wealthy during the '20s, he died $30,000 in debt in 1933. Titus went to Edison Junior High and Fremont High School. He remains a walking encyclopedia of local history and he told me several anecdotes about his long life in Florence-Firestone. Titus said that there were so many fires at Goodyear Tire Company in his youth that Goodyear had its own Fire Department. He also spoke about the high level of toxic chemicals that were in the area because of all the factories. He reminisced about the Pacific Electric Streetcar and told me,

"The deaths we have had on the Blue Line are in the same places they were back in the days of the Red Car. History repeats itself." Titus also told me about the long-gone Gentry Theater that was at 66th and Compton Avenue, and about how one of the first Carl's Junior that ever opened was on Florence and Central. Titus has seen the neighborhood through all its ups and downs. He told me that for a time over two decades ago there were "20 dope dealers 24 hours a day," standing outside on his street. He said that sometimes he would find drugs that dealers would hide in his mailbox. Following a drive-by shooting next to his house in 1993, the sheriffs slowly began to clean up his street. They made it a one-way road and now he tells me it is much safer.

Titus told me that he did not become involved in local community issues until the late 1980s, and it was the desperate nature of the times that pulled him in. He has collaborated with the Florence-Firestone Community Leaders and is well-known by the stakeholders as the District's elder statesman. In recent years, his sister Mary Rose Cortese has also moved back to the area and works closely with him around the community. On the night of the site launch, he was warmly greeted by other longtime residents like William Allen.

One more engaged local advocate I met was John Jones III, a field deputy from the 15th District that works for councilmember Joe Buscaino. Jones grew up in Florence-Firestone and now works in Watts for the City of Los Angeles. He told me he started as an activist in his teen years when he was involved with the preservation of Roosevelt Park. In 2008, Jones founded the Eastside Riders (ESR), a local bicycle club based in Watts and South Los Angeles. According to their website, "The purpose of the ESR is to prevent youth from joining gangs and/or taking drugs, but also engage youth who have a desire to enrich the community through recreational activities, specifically focusing on bicycle riding." The night

I met Jones, he was also talking with Jonathan P. Bell about a series of proposed bike lanes that will connect from Florence-Firestone into Watts.

A few nights after the launch, I took a drive around Florence-Firestone with Jonathan P. Bell. He drove me down Slauson and showed me the old concrete platforms that remained on the street from when the Pacific Electric Streetcar was there. He drove me past a new pocket park on Gage, adjacent to the Blue Line Station. He also showed me where the first Sheriff's Station once was at Firestone Park near Nadeau and Compton Avenue. The building remains there but it is now the Sheriffs Youth Activity League, a place dedicated to helping local youth. Bell drove me past the County Library on Florence near Miramonte, and told me that he wrote a thesis proposal on the history of the Florence and Graham branch libraries a few years ago. They are two of the oldest libraries in the County system, but have had very little history recorded about either one. Bell is also not a fan of the idea some have of calling South Los Angeles "SOLA." Similar to Teka-Lark Fleming and Skira Martinez, to him the area will always be South Central Los Angeles, and any new name erases the area's early history. Furthermore, he notes, "Sola in Spanish means lonely girl," and for Bell, the vibrant streets of Florence-Firestone are anything but lonely. He loves the bustling shops on Florence Avenue and the district's colorful murals. He also showed me a few beautiful old craftsman homes nestled within the fabric of the neighborhood.

The Office of Supervisor Mark Ridley Thomas in the Second District commissioned Cal Arts Provost Jeannene Przyblyski to do a history project on Florence-Firestone. Last year, they also commissioned writer and artist Rosten Woo to do a highly acclaimed project on the nearby area of Willowbrook that came out on Half Letter Press, who will also be publishing the project on Florence-Firestone.

Bell is excited to be taking over as the new incoming volunteer project manager for the Florence-Firestone "Everyday Heroes," project because the former project manager Angel Nicolas has now become the Community Library Manager in Lynwood. There are many more residents and community leaders' narratives that Bell intends to film and record. Bell is the perfect man for this job because he's been working in the area for a dozen years and he's well acquainted with residents and business owners.

Bell and other community leaders like William Allen, Paula Trejo, Rick Aldridge, Gloria Medina, Erica Ortega, Celica Quinones, and Arthur Jones are firmly committed to improving the conditions of Florence-Firestone. The area has come a long way over the last century and has dramatically improved in the last decade because of their efforts. Salute to these everyday heroes and to Florence-Firestone for being a historic and vibrant district in the landscape of L.A. Letters.

Los Angeles:
the Land of 1000 Dances

Though it was settled in 1781
under Spanish rule
The first settlers of Los Angeles
were Mexicans, Mestizos..
People of mixed ancestry..
26 of the 44 original pobladores
were also part African..
The City of Angels
has always been Afrolatin
Mexican & African together
since the beginning.
Aztlan is America,
America is Aztlan
Los Angeles is the Land of 1000 dances.

1.
Most of the barrios in East L.A.
are along the floodplain
before the river was put in concrete
heavy rains would put the streets
a few feet under water..
The same is true in South Central,
they used to call Watts Mud Town...
Put the poor people DOWN
in the flood plain
keep the wealthy in the hills
Watts to East Los..

2.

Crossing the 6th street bridge
listening to Cisco kid
It's a thin line between love & hate
Why can't we be friends?
Don't listen to the television
Television talks about division..
we are one people, besides
everybody kicks it to Wilson Pickett
forget the differences
Music is the bridge..

3.

Generations of car clubs cruising
to the same radio stations
underground bootlegs
love songs & ballads..
Art Laboe low riders oldies show
Doo wop--pachuco hop, pompadours, corridos,
Johnny Otis, El Chicano,
Brown Brothers of Soul
War, Santana & Tower of Power..
Afrolatin percussion All day music
Bailar la bamba, Whittier Boulevard
Do the Slauson
The eastside sound came from R&B soul
Sam Cooke & Nat King Cole..

4.

East L.A garage bands flipped the script
with their own twist &
started the Chicano soul movement..
Huggy Boy was the Eastside Casey Kasem,
the scene multiplied after Richie Valens died..
Valens was a leviathan.

He was born Richard Valenzuela in Paicoma,
he rocked international by 19,
generations of local musicians
followed his footsteps..
Eastside kings like Cannibal & the Headhunters,
Thee Midnighters, the Carlos Brothers,
Ruben Guevarra, Ruben & the Jets, Rampart Records,
the Village Callers, Brothers of SouL,
Tiarra, Ernie Perez, Sabor! Brotherhood is the message
black & brown unity
together since the beginning..

5.
Music is the bridge! Wassup rockers!
Punk rock Chicanos carry on a legacy
of generations of homegrown music
Lonely, lonely nights
low riding in Lincoln Heights
all the way to Aliso Village,
Lorena under the bridge, Montebello,
the El Monte Legion Stadium, Hollenbeck Park
City Terrace, Mariachi Plaza,
Tire shops, taco trucks, Que onda huero?
Olympic, Atlantic, Soto, El Sereno
the Sears Tower & General Hospital,
East L.A. goes a long way
like its Cousin South Central.

6.
Anthony Quinn was born Anthony Quinones
he grew up in Boyle Heights..
He was Mexican even if he played
Zorba the Greek..

Mobster Mickey Cohen grew up in Boyle Heights
it was also Japanese & Jewish.

And now Brooklyn Avenue is
named Caesar Chavez,
Several Buddhist temples
still exist like the Rissho Kosei Kai..

7.
Original cholo lettering dating back
to the Roaring 20s
was L.A. first graffiti
Muralists from LA RAZA are
L.A. Art pioneers like Chaz, Gronk & Eloy Torres
Self Help Graphics, the Chicano movement
of Art & Soul, Looms large in L.A. lore!
Historic like Central Avenue, Laurel Canyon,
surf music, Venice beats, the punk scene,
generations of local musicians puttin it down..
Here's one for the Eastside Sound...
The Brighter side of Darkness
Soul Communicators, Jackie Wilson & the Drifters,
the Dramatics, the Stylistics, the Whispers,
Johnny Guitar Watson, Crystal Blue Persuasion,
Joe Bataan the Afro-Filipino,
just an ordinary guy
Telling it like it is,
Don't listen to the television
Television talks about division
We are one people.

8.
It comes back to harmony
Si Se Puede
Music is the heartbeat
Whatcha see is what you get
Are you lookin for real lovin?!
The answer is in the music

Be thankful for what you've got
Respect to Ruben Salazar
& the Chicano Moratorium
Freedom fighters! Luis Rodriguez,
Busstop Prophet, Ulises Diaz, Quetzal,
Los Lobos, Burning Star, Crewest, Mark Gonzales,
Chicano roots & culture!

9.
Aztlan is America..
America is Aztlan
Brown the color of creation..
The Eastside Soundsystem
Los Angeles Bridges,
Black & Brown unity
together since the beginning!
Music is the heartbeat

10.
Build the bridge
lay down the bricks
fill in the ridges
stack the sticks
feed the fire
consider the cost
take it up higher
the city is ours!!

Forget the differences..
Los Angeles is the Land of 1000 dances....

The Hills Are Alive in City Terrace

Boyle Heights and East Los Angeles are both known the world over for their important place in Chicano history. A lesser known but equally important area of East Los Angeles is City Terrace. Like Boyle Heights, City Terrace has a fascinating history and is also a mecca for murals. This essay examines City Terrace with a special focus on its geography, cultural history, activist legacy and the many murals throughout the area.

City Terrace is the area directly north of Boyle Heights, south of Cal State Los Angeles and just west of Alhambra and Monterey Park. The neighborhood's defining geographic features are its many hills and the hundreds of homes that cascade the topography. A transitional area exists between Boyle Heights and City Terrace along Wabash Street where a former Jewish Community Center is now the Salesian Boys and Girls Club. Wabash turns into City Terrace Drive adjacent to this site.

Arts activist and writer Tomas Benitez explains further, "Wabash connected Boyle Heights with City Terrace but it was over the hill. They were two different areas, City Terrace being the 'nicer' part. It is parallel to the 10 Freeway and the other side of the hills from Brooklyn, later Cesar Chavez Avenue. It was the back door, the road that only the locals knew and used."

The heart of City Terrace was first developed in the early 1920s by Walter Leimert, a few years before the Leimert family developed Leimert Park in the late 1920s. Originally known as a Jewish neighborhood, like Boyle Heights, it also had a small Russian and Japanese population along with Mexican residents. Driving through City Terrace today there are traces of this past, like a three-story building on City Terrace Drive that has a Star of David near the top of the structure's façade.

Arts Legacy

I drove around City Terrace many times both on my own and with two longtime residents: First with Sesshu Foster, the author of the great book "City Terrace Field Manual," and later with Tomas Benitez. Both lived many years of their lives in City Terrace. They each pointed out hidden sites I never would have found without their assistance. Both attended Wilson High School in nearby El Sereno and they each came of age during the time of the Chicano Moratorium. Before sharing some of their anecdotes, I'd like to begin with a few City Terrace tales told to me by Los Angeles Poet Laureate Luis Rodriguez.

Luis Rodriguez spent much of his life in L.A.'s Eastside and he lived in City Terrace during the 1970s. "City Terrace when I lived there was all barrio--no sidewalks, dirt roads, with ravines, hills, vacant lots, old homes," Rodriguez remembers. "My first wife, Camila, grew up there on Herbert. We were 'high school' sweethearts." Camila had gone to Garfield High and though Rodriguez did not, he met her while working as a political organizer for the Movimiento Estudiantil Chicano de Aztlan (MEChA).

Rodriguez says that at the time, City Terrace was the neighborhood that looked most like his own barrio of Las Lomas in South San Gabriel. "In the early 1970s, both barrios were poor as all get out," he notes. Rodriguez lived at the end of Geraghty Street, where it becomes Bostwick. Rodriguez also lived in City Terrace a few years later when he worked for the Eastside Sun (Eastern Group Publications) and later when he had an office in the old Self-Help Graphics building on Chavez and Gage.

"City Terrace was always full of life--people on the streets, noises, fights at times, glass breaking. But it was mostly good families, hard-working people, almost entirely Mexican although there were a few remnants of the Jewish families that once predominated, some Asians, other whites." Rodriguez notes that much has changed in 40 years. "You can still see the rundown homes, the vacant lots, the sidewalk-less streets, although almost everything is now paved, and new homes have sprouted up here and there. There are efforts to gentrify--make this place palatable to well-off, mostly white, people. But for now, it's still heavily Mexican, still barrio, still one of L.A. most interesting neighborhoods," he says.

Rodriguez loves to take visitors to a hill on De Garmo off Pomeroy where you can see the downtown skyscrapers and miles of the Eastside. It's one of the best views of the city from any direction. "People from all over love it when I take them there," he tells me. Coincidentally on the day we spoke, Rodriguez was just returning from there after giving some visitors a taste of the Eastside.

In continuation of my trip through City Terrace, Sesshu Foster took me on a thorough drive one afternoon and showed me just about every corner of City Terrace in less than three hours. Foster grew up in City Terrace from the time he was in early elementary school until he went to college. His mom still lives in the house he grew up in and she has been there over 50 years. Foster took me to meet her and the view from her backyard was like the one Rodriguez describes above.

Foster's book, *City Terrace Field Manual* from Kaya Press, is a collection of prose poems that capture the neighborhood in technicolor. The book combines urban realism with surrealism mixing his childhood memories with various musings. "I have my friends and we have our own world in the streets of City Terrace, East L.A.," he writes. *City Terrace Field Manual*, is considered one of the greatest works ever composed about the Eastside. Foster's work paved the way for a whole generation of Eastside poets. One of them is Jessica Ceballos, who was born in City Terrace in 1977 and currently organizes the Bluebird Poetry Reading Series at Avenue 50 Gallery. She recalls first reading *City Terrace Field Manual* when she was 20 years old and the reality was made concrete. "Stories I had heard were retold, through someone else's lens, but as their own," she says. "We lived the same lives, but the fractures were in different parts of the body. In this book, the entirety of Los Angeles wasn't neglected, it was honored, told from the hills of City Terrace."

Foster showed me multiple murals including Willie Herrón's well-known 1972 mural, "The Wall that Cracked Open." We drove me down the alley where it is located, along with many other murals, just north of City Terrace Drive. Foster told me the history behind each and how the art movement he grew up around in City Terrace influenced him. Foster was a few years behind Herrón at Wilson High School and the spirit that Herrón injected into his murals inspired Foster to become an activist. Furthermore, Foster says Herrón's commitment to social justice with his collective ASCO greatly informed the ethos behind his books like *City Terrace Field Manual*.

One of the only people in Los Angeles who know as much about murals of City Terrace as Foster is Isabel Rojas-Williams, the Executive Director of the Los Angeles Mural Conservancy. She notes that the murals in City Terrace were inspired by Jose Clemente Orozco, Diego Rivera, and David Alfaro Siqueiros, the three great Mexican muralists from the 1920s and '30s.

"Pioneer muralists inspired by the 'Three Greats,' like Willie Herrón, Johnny Gonzalez, and George Yepes helped give birth to the 1970's Chicano Mural Movement by painting iconic murals in City Terrace," says Rojas-Williams. Both she and Foster recounted how Herrón painted "The Wall that Cracked

Open," after his younger brother was stabbed there by local gang members. Herrón grew up in City Terrace and his family owned Macias Bakery on City Terrace Drive. The mural was painted in the alley behind the bakery.

Rojas-Williams told me that this section of City Terrace Drive has become known as "Callejón Herrón," because Herrón painted several pieces over a three block stretch of the street. These pieces include, "Quetzalcoatl, the Aztec god, symbolized as a plumed serpent," also from 1972 and a mural he painted in 1976, "La Doliente de Hidalgo." In 2011, he painted "Asco: East of No West," for the Getty's Pacific Standard Time Initiative. Williams calls it "Herrón's monument to ASCO, the avant-garde art collective he co-founded in the 1970s."

A few blocks west of "Callejón Herrón," is a mural by George Yepes on the exterior of a church. Painted in 1992, the work is called, "Pieta del Tepeyac." The work depicts, "a traditional Madonna and Child next to an image of a mother cradling her fallen gang-member son," explains Rojas-Williams. A few steps from the Yepes mural at the City Terrace Library is a ceramic tile mural created by José Luis Gonzalez, the co-founder of Goez Art Studios. The 1978 piece titled "Ofrenda Maya I (Mayan Offering I)" is done in Pre-Columbian style and depicts Mayan warriors.

These iconic murals have made City Terrace a place that art aficionados from all over the world visit. According to Rojas-Williams, "Herrón, Yepes, and González symbolize the spirit, which guided the 1970's Chicano muralists. Their artworks were then, and are still today, tools of social activism, of empowerment, communication, and education for the people of City Terrace and all who often tour the murals of this unique neighborhood."

Sesshu Foster is particularly fond of Paul Botello's mural at City Terrace Park. He pointed out how there were no graffiti tags on it at all. Titled "Inner Resources," the piece emits a psychedelic peaceful spirit that Botello says is, "about the veneration of life." The central figure is a Mexican Indian goddess surrounded by people planting, harvesting and celebrating. Botello is a native of East Los Angeles.

The contemporary artist Jose Ramirez still lives in City Terrace. Best known for his mural at White Memorial Hospital, his father's family lived there in the 1960s. When he was born in 1967, they lived on City Terrace Drive. Over the years, he has painted the houses on hills with views of Downtown Los Angeles. Ramirez is deeply involved with the local community participating in events, classes and workshops at Self Help Graphics, Plaza de la Raza, Casa 0101, the Eastside Cafe and other cultural art spaces that are in Boyle Heights, Lincoln Heights, El Sereno and Downtown. Ramirez loves being in the middle of "Aztlan." He also loves the large lots. "I have expanded my art/work into the garden and have developed my south facing lot into 'a perennial edible garden (food forest),'" he says. I was at his home and his sprawling garden was truly something to behold.

Activism

Another Eastside luminary with a deep connection to City Terrace is the former director of Self Help Graphics and longtime Chicano activist Tomas Benitez. Benitez lived for many years of his childhood across the street from City Terrace Park. His mom, Linda Benitez Basco, was a local activist that founded the East Los Angeles Community Center, a small NPO that was deeply involved in neighborhood politics. She was instrumental in the expansion of the City Terrace Park and getting the tennis courts built. Today, Benitez is trying to have the tennis courts named after his mom.

Benitez was also strongly connected to the park because he grew up playing baseball there. "When I moved to City Terrace I joined the Little League and got my first full uniform," Benitez remembers. He played second base and right field with the Orioles. In recent years, Benitez has written a lot about the Chicano connection to baseball in Los Angeles and this all started back in his childhood at City Terrace Park.

Mrs. Benitez Baca worked closely with several other leaders and residents in East Los Angeles, often inviting them to her home. She would often host dinners "with Ed Elliot who was the County Supervisor and lived around the corner up Miller Drive." The conversations over food at their house helped transform the neighborhood. The pioneering Chicano congressman Ed Roybal would also eat over at their house. His mom would make her specialty, steak picado. "Ed would always come by to have a plate." These meals were instrumental to the expanded development of City Terrace Park.

Benitez carried on his mother's legacy of activism and participated in the Chicano Moratorium on August 29th, 1970 shortly after he graduated from Wilson High. He remembers the dramatic events of the Moratorium vividly:

> "Mom and I went to the Moratorium together, but it was hot, so she took my little brother home. I was working crowd control in the park, a newly recruited volunteer. I heard there was a disturbance a block away but the event was going on well, so we kept the perimeter in the park in check, making sure people were being well behaved. In a flash, the cops moved in and formed a line across from us, which agitated the crowd. We were trying to hold them at bay, telling them not to throw things. The cops advanced then charged and all hell broke loose. We were the first ones struck as they shot gas over us. I got trampled but not busted. I got up and tried to get out of the park but the cops had blocked the street. The only way was through the park so I ran into the

gas, still trying to get away."

"For the first time in my life I felt pride in being a Chicano walking down the street, then in a moment it was all mayhem. I heard cops' cars pulling up on the street but I did not turn around. Kept on walking... I cut through side streets and stayed away from signals. I made it to my Dad's office on First."

Benitez spent the next week laying low at his mom's house across the street from City Terrace Park. That fall he began attending school at Los Angeles City College. He now lives less than a mile south of City Terrace near Obregon Park.

This experience led Benitez into a lifetime of activism that continues 45 years later. Benitez also shared memories about the Floral Drive-In Movie Theater. The theater was on the eastern border of City Terrace and Monterey Park. During the years it operated, the land was Unincorporated Los Angeles County and considered East Los Angeles. The site is now a part of Monterey Park and a corporate office park is there, but for many years it was a large drive-in that showed films in Spanish. Though it closed in 1986, Benitez saw many films there in the 1970s and early '80s. The combination of unique houses and rolling topography give City Terrace a distinct charm within the landscape of Los Angeles. Nestled deep in its alleys and canyons are murals, sculptures, funky houses and colorful gardens. A great example is the big cactus garden on Floral just east of Eastern. A great way to sample this epic area is to either read Sesshu Foster's *City Terrace Field Manual*, or drive down City Terrace Drive. Salute to City Terrace for being one of the most fascinating pockets in the geography of L.A. Letters.

OTOMISAN: THE LAST JAPANESE RESTAURANT IN BOYLE HEIGHTS

Otomisan is the only remaining Japanese Restaurant in Boyle Heights. Decades ago the now heavily-Latino neighborhood was home to a large Japanese population, partly due to its proximity to Little Tokyo, and there are still traces of that community that remains.

Founded in 1956, the restaurant can still be found at its original location on East First Street, two blocks east of Soto. Sixty-two years later, the warm mojo of the small dining area radiates the Japanese tradition of Boyle Heights and calls you back for another tasty plate.

This is a story of family, food and neighborhood.

Yayoi Watanabe bought the restaurant seven years ago. She had already owned a dry cleaner in Boyle Heights for 15 years on 4th and Fresno. Her 30-year old daughter Judy Hayashi reminisces, "I remember always going next door to Fuji Cafe and getting some good Japanese (like home cooking)."

Fuji Café on 4th Street was one of the last remaining Japanese family eateries in Boyle Heights. When it closed after one of the owners died, Watanabe became motivated to keep Boyle Heights' Japanese tradition alive.

When one of the owners of Otomisan died a few years later and it went up for sale, Watanabe decided to buy the place and keep it open. She didn't want it to disappear like the Fuji Café, which became a Mexican restaurant.

The coziness of the space makes you feel the generations of family that have come through the doors. Between the Japanese retirement home up the street and Boyle Heights locals, the diner-style booths and counter seats stay close to full, serving up family style comfort food—an authentic mom and pop restaurant alive in the 21st Century.

Judy works with her mother one day a week. Her father was a pioneer in the restaurant supply industry, having introduced hot towels to dining tables around Little Tokyo. Judy—who grew up with her family in the Virgil Village area, where many Japanese had lived in the 1970s—spent much of her youth driving with her father from restaurant to restaurant, delivering the hot new product.

Bilingual in Japanese and English with a charismatic demeanor, Judy became well known in the community as an invaluable asset to any place she worked; her versatility made her a face for Little Tokyo. Her success is not surprising, since her mother had also spent much of her time working in Little Tokyo from the 1970s on, until she started her dry cleaner business in Boyle Heights.

The connection between Boyle Heights and Little Tokyo runs down First Street. "The Japanese people that worked in Little Tokyo used to live in Boyle Heights," Hayashi says. "It was kind of like an extension of Little Tokyo. Even now, there are still Japanese and Nikkei's living in the area."

One of them is her own mother, who lives a few blocks east of the restaurant near the Evergreen Cemetery and the Rissho Kosei Kei Buddhist Temple. Watanabe lives close enough to walk to work. She loves Boyle Heights and won't be moving away anytime soon.

Eastside diners are ecstatic that she's sticking around— Otomisan serves classic traditional Japanese food in an otherwise mostly Latino neighborhood. The cozy eatery feels like a window that time forgot. The food and ambience leads customers like 38-year-old East Hollywood native Ken Montenegro to keep coming back. On the way out the door, before thanking Ms. Watanabe, he told us he's been coming for years now.

Judy reminisces with her mother and shares memories of Little Tokyo. They remember a time when Nisei Week meant that the streets would be virtually impossible to walk through due to the dense crowd of visitors. It was also a place of comfort, a home away from home for many Japanese transplants as well as Japanese Americans.

"I always thought Little Tokyo was a representation of our history here in L.A," Judy says. "It was a place where the people from Japan could still celebrate where they came from and the Japanese culture. I remember walking down the street and all you could hear was mostly the Japanese language. I remember more Japanese restaurants than there are now."

Times change especially in the age of corporate chains and luxury condos. These changes make places like Otomisan that much more important. "I hope we never forget the history behind Little Tokyo and Boyle Heights," Judy says.

Japanese Boyle Heights in the 21st Century

For over 80 years, every summer in early August the annual Nisei Week Parade takes place in Little Tokyo. The Japanese community in Little Tokyo is directly linked to Boyle Heights via East First Street, and over the years many residents of the eastside community have made the trek over the First Street Bridge to the festival. In the previous essay, I wrote about Otomisan, the last remaining Japanese restaurant in Boyle Heights. Located on East First Street since the 1950s, they are a part of a small handful of Japanese churches, a school, and florist that have remained in the area from the early-20th century. This piece spotlights three remaining Japanese spaces clustered within a block of each other on First Street in Boyle Heights: the Rissho Kosei-kai Buddhist Temple, Tenrikyo Church, and Rafu Chuo Gakuen, the Japanese school on Saratoga Street. Like Otomisan, these venerated spaces have a longstanding history and intimate connection with the Boyle Heights Japanese community.

The Rissho Kosei-kai

The Rissho Kosei-kai Buddhist Temple is on First and Mott Street, just a few blocks east of Otomisan. Nestled between Mott and the Tenrikyo Church directly east, the Rissho Kosei-kai is one of the most popular sects of Japanese Buddhism. Within the congregation are not only a mix of many longtime Japanese residents from Boyle Heights and Japanese-Americans from all over Southern California, but members also include a cohort of multicultural Angelenos who practice their faith there.

The site and building where the Rissho Kosei-kai is located was originally built in 1926 for Higashi Honganji, one of the oldest sects of Japanese Buddhism. After 50 years in Boyle Heights, they moved to Little Tokyo and sold their structure to the Rissho-Kosei-kai in 1976. The current assistant reverend Ken Nagata was a part of a team that renovated the space. He tells me, "Rissho Kosei-kai of Los Angeles is a place where Buddhism is learned and practiced. Our focus of Buddhism is the Lotus Sutra and it encompasses the wholesomeness of Buddha's effort in his life since it was taught near the end of his career."

A longtime member, the 84-year-old Dr. James Hodgkin, told me about a 2005 *National Geographic* article on the growth of Buddhism around the world. Hodgkin says, "While reporting an upbeat and positive picture of the growth of Buddhism globally, the reporter concluded that Buddhism was 'losing its appeal' in Japan. Accepting an offer to see where the 'heart of Japanese Buddhism is still beating,' the reporter was taken to the Headquarters of the Rissho Kosei-kai." The essay noted that the Rissho Kosei-kai continues to grow at a rate faster than other sects of Japanese Buddhism.

Hodgkin credits the growth "to the vision and wisdom of Founder Nikkyo Niwano, who applied knowledge and practice of the Lotus Sutra in a new and effective way." Though the specific precepts are too numerous to detail here, one of the key components of the Rissho Kosei-kai is "the hoza circle." The hoza circle concludes the Sunday service and members sit together in a circle to share everyday experiences and any problems, sufferings, worries, anxieties and questions whether they are big or small. The dialogue is multigenerational and non-hierarchal. This openness has made many newcomers feel very welcome.

Twenty-six-year-old Migel Armas is a lifelong member of the Rissho Kosei-kai. His parents were married there back in the 1980s. Though he grew up in the San Fernando Valley, his own ancestry epitomizes the history of Boyle Heights. His father was raised in a Catholic family in Mexico and his mother was raised Buddhist in Japan. They met in Los Angeles and found a home together at the Rissho Kosei-kai. Every year Armas participates in the Nisei Week Parade, and he tells me, "I have been coming since I was born, growing up with the youth and the older kids there." Sometime during high school, he really began to learn the teachings.

In recent years the Rissho Kosei-kai's congregation has grown to include many from the younger generation. Twenty-four-year old Richard Kano grew up in Montebello and East Los Angeles. Kano found Buddhism in his early 20s after he burned out on the party scene. He says, "Rissho Kosei-kai taught me how to walk the practical path of the Buddha. The middle way, I have rediscovered purpose again and compassion for myself and others by following the bodhisattva way." A multicultural and multigenerational fellowship joins Kano every week. Kano credits practicing Buddhism with reinvigorating his life and refreshing his senses. "The other big obstacle I had was seeing beauty. I only saw struggle and pain in everything," he shares; "but the practice of reciting the Lotus Sutra, being a part of the sangha (the fellowship), and having gratitude and humility for all things has shown me the Buddha nature within myself. We are taught if I change myself, I change the world."

Kano's joyful spirit is corroborated by the head Reverend in Los Angeles, T. Yoshizawa who says, "We wish to share this powerful and positive energy with everyone in Los Angeles." To this end, the doors are open to all and they always welcome new members. The Rissho-Kosei-kai participates every year in the Nisei Week Parade. The night before they hold an annual barbeque and celebrate with the congregation.

Tenrikyo

Tenrikyo Church is also located on First Street, just east of the Rissho Kosei-kai and just west of Saratoga Street. Tenrikyo is a monotheistic religion that began in Japan in the early 19th Century. They recently celebrated their 80th anniversary in America. Their anniversary celebration was attended by several hundred people, and their church continues to attract not only Japanese in the immediate area, but also many different people from across Southern California. Their North American headquarters is the Boyle Heights space. Ikuyo Yuge is a lifelong Tenrikyo member who was born in 1937 on site, and a lifelong resident of Boyle Heights who attended First Street Elementary, Hollenbeck Middle School and Roosevelt High School. Yuge was also a professor at UCLA for two decades and has lived for many years on Boyle Avenue. Her father in law was one of the first seven Japanese to receive the $20,000 reparations in 1989 for being interned during World War II.

A photo of Yuge and her father in law celebrating this moment remains on exhibit at the Japanese-American National Museum. He was 102 years old at the time and she accompanied him to Washington D.C. to receive it. She tells me that though he died about a week after the trip, at least he received some redemption just before he passed. Yuge's sons are also involved with Tenrikyo. Her son Michael Yuge runs the Tenrikyo New York Center and her son Robert Yuge is the Editor of the Tenrikyo newsletter and a vital member of the Boyle Heights headquarters.

Yuge also tells me that their original location was near Hollenbeck Park on Cummings Street. She also said that across the street from Tenrikyo's current location, where the Food for Less now stands, was once the church, "Little Sisters of the Poor." The old church's bell tower top sits in the middle of the parking lot, commemorating the history of the now-gone holy site. Tenrikyo organizes many events throughout the year, like their "Family Festival" to promote brotherhood and spiritual growth. Furthermore, they participate every year in the Nisei Week Parade as well.

Rafu Chuo Gakuen

In addition to his involvement in Tenrikyo, Robert Yuge is also the Director of the Parent-Teacher Association at the Japanese School across the street, otherwise known as the Rafu Chuo Gakuen. The Rafu Chuo Gakuen, located on Saratoga Street across from Tenrikyo, operates on Saturdays teaching both the Japanese language and traditional customs to Japanese children up to their late teen years. One of the close associates of the school, Matthew Mori, shared with me the school's extensive background story and its longstanding history in the neighborhood.

Mori has a wealth of knowledge about the history of both the school and Japanese Boyle Heights in general. He told me, "Tokiwa Gakuen was founded in February 1929 by Mr. Gunpei Kuroyanagi, Mrs. Reiko Kawakami, Mr. Tsurujiro Yamada, and others at Higashi Hongwanji. At the time (1926-1976), Higashi Honganji was located at 118 North Mott Street —now part of the Rissho Kosei-kai Center." He explains more, "Tokiwa Gakuen and Higashi Hongwanji purchased a school bus together in September 1929, and by October of the same year, the school was moved to South Saratoga Street and renamed Boyle Heights Chuo Gakuen by Mr. Kesagoro Umekubo. The school was moved to its present location in February 1932, a new school bus was acquired, and the school was renamed Rafu Chuo Gakuen."

Over the years the school has continued to evolve and progress. Mori says the school was a part of a larger collection of Japanese schools across the Southland. He says, "According to Mrs. Hatsue Yamaguchi, in 1936, there were over 200 Japanese schools in Southern California, and Rafu Chuo Gakuen was 'one of the most prestigious schools, second only to Compton Gakuen.' (Established in 1924, Compton Gakuen—together with Moneta Gakuen [1912] and Gardena Gakuen [1915]—were precursors to the present-day Gardena Valley Japanese Cultural Institute's Nihongo Gakuen.) During World War II the school was interrupted and classes did not resume until 1947.

Mori shares, "The Chuo Gakuen campus was used to temporarily house the 'Terminal Islanders' during the wartime relocation and internment of Japanese Americans. 'Non-Japanese immigrants' lived at the school during the war and their eviction was apparently a contentious affair." Following the war in 1951, Rafu Chuo Gakuen became an affiliate of Kyodo System (established in 1948 as a kind of "Unified Japanese Language School System"). The school continued to grow and the campus was expanded and improved through the 1960s and '70s.

In addition to telling me about the school, Mori also informed me about the Maryknoll Family, another historic group of Japanese-Americans on the Eastside. He says, "Maryknoll was a Japanese Catholic parish in the 'Loft District' just east of Little Tokyo. My wife and I were both born in Boyle Heights. She grew up on Boyle Avenue and attended both Maryknoll School and Chuo Gakuen." By the time Mori and his wife had kids, the Maryknoll School no longer existed as they knew it. For this reason and more, they are glad to have their children attend Japanese school in Boyle Heights. He shares, "I think Chuo Gakuen helps my family maintain a connection to the place and the people and the culture my wife and I grew up with."

Toshi Kayama is another parent with children that attend the school. Kayama sees the program as more than just a language institute, but "as a valuable investment in our children's future." He also says, "Japanese schools give our children the opportunity to make more friends, learn important Japanese traditions and values, and even develop a deeper understanding and appreciation for Japanese culture." Kayama and his wife know it's a serious commitment for their children to sacrifice their Saturday, but "they hope their efforts will pay off as they become truly bilingual and bi-cultural, embracing both their American and Japanese heritage, values, and culture."

There are a few other vestiges of Japanese Boyle Heights that still stand. Besides Otomisan, a few blocks east of Rafu Chuo Gakuen on First Street is the Konko Church and the Haru Florist. On Fourth and Saratoga, there is also the Nichiren Buddhist Temple. The historic legacy of Japanese Boyle Heights remains vibrant in these spaces.

A key component of Japanese religion and culture is the idea of ancestor veneration, essentially the idea of gratitude to your family and specifically appreciating one's ancestors. This concept is especially expressed during Obon, which has been called "the Japanese Day of the Dead." The Obon Festival occurs in July and August throughout Southern California in Little Tokyo and Boyle Heights, and at other various sites, including most Japanese churches. Furthermore, the Nisei Week Parade is always concluded by the "Obon Dance" along First Street. The parade is usually held on the second Sunday in August from 4 to 7 p.m. in Little Tokyo. Salute to Nisei Week, these sites and the Rissho Kosei-kai, Tenrikyo and the Rafu Chuo Gakuen for being monumental historic locations in the landscape of L.A. Letters.

Homage to Little Tokyo

*(Over the last 20 years I've spent many nights
& days in Little Tokyo, this poem is my tribute)*

Little Tokyo is Los Angeles's
second oldest community
the cultural spine runs between
First and Second Street, bonded
by community history, common ancestry
& the legacy of internment
The Japanese American National Museum
is a nexus

Little Tokyo is undergoing transformation.
The specter of gentrification, rising rents
& cookie cutter condos continues to alter
the original footprint
The size has transitioned
but development will never kill
the vision or the district's defining spirit.

The boundaries transcend geography:
Little Tokyo is Obon dancing
in the middle of First Street.
Little Tokyo is a cultural grounding
George Abe playing flute under
the grapefruit tree browsing books
at the AmerAsian bookstore

Little Tokyo is traci kato-kiriyama taking the stage
at the Aratani Theater or Jason Arimoto

on Ukulele singing passionately:
Let My love surround you

Little Tokyo is FandangObon bridging Japanese,
Mexican & African American communities
Little Tokyo is over a thousand people
dancing down Halldale in Gardena
on a hot August evening
Little Tokyo is a cruise down Alameda
pedal with the Eastside Riders
down Central Avenue
through the corridor to the Watts Towers

Little Tokyo is Bronzeville,
Charlie Parker blowing on First Street
Little Tokyo is Scott Kurashige writing
about *The Shifting Grounds of Race,*
the Crenshaw District was once the largest
Japanese neighborhood in America
The birthplace of Yellow Brotherhood & *Gidra*

Little Tokyo is the Poetry of Amy Uyematsu
the prose of Naomi Hirahara, the photography
of Mike Murase, the haiku of Rubén Guevara,
Little Tokyo is the sacred song of the Sangha
chanting *Namo Myo-ho Renge Kyo*

Little Tokyo is the Japanese Village Plaza,
Toyo Miyatake's camera,
a pitcher of cold Asahi beer,
Noguchi's sculpture,
Little Tokyo is skaters rail sliding
in the courtyard
Little Tokyo is the *Go For Broke Memorial*,
Suehiro Cafe, Fugetsu-Do, Monzo's Udon
Noodle's, Katsu Don from Curry House,

an izakaya on the corner,
four food trucks on First,
Shop, share, support
Little Tokyo is legacy businesses,
Nisei witnesses

Little Tokyo is Boyle Heights across
the First Street bridge.
There were once wildflowers
on the edge of the Wolfskill Orchard
Little Tokyo is taiko drumming
a long list of lullabies redefining courage

Little Tokyo is *Transpacific Borderlands*, the art
of the Japanese Diaspora in Lima, Los Angeles,
Mexico City & São Paulo
Little Tokyo is Yayoi Kusama's
Infinity Mirrors

Little Tokyo is Emi Motokawa crocheting
Kokeshi dolls, Little Tokyo is Eka Loa
& Skye Ren eating shaved ice at Mikawaya

Little Tokyo is Scott Oshima at
Sustainable Little Tokyo preserving history
Little Tokyo is Kristin Fukushima at
The Little Tokyo Community Council
protecting the district from financial predators
looking to take a piece of the neighborhood

Little Tokyo is the Little Tokyo
Service Center serving the
Center of the district with
intergenerational coalitions
sustaining the civic legacy
through people power & policy

Even if the eastern section of Little Tokyo
attempts to call itself the Arts District
with luxury condos now leasing
The energy of the enclave
will never be destroyed,
the song remains the embodiment,
a sort of anchoring

Little Tokyo is Manzanar,
Little Tokyo is Nisei gardeners &
J-A Nurseries before the interstate
Little Tokyo is the Japanese American
Cultural Center, Little Tokyo
is youth basketball on Saturday
in the Budokan with a 38,000
square foot mezzanine
Little Tokyo is California Oak wine
barrels, the tree is over 150 years old

Little Tokyo is a Japanese folk song,
pounding rice, sifting grain, holding hands
with nothing to fear. *If you're gonna be*
a fool, you might as well dance
Little Tokyo is Los Angeles

Frequently Asked Questions

There is no question that Los Angeles is a fragmented metropolis. Many urban theorists have used terms like "spatial apartheid" and "Balkanization," to characterize the sometimes explosive race relations and segregated neighborhoods of the Southland. Longtime Angelinos know that there is a split between East and West Los Angeles. What about South Central, the Valley, Long Beach, Orange County & the Inland Empire? Here's a breakdown for the record.

Where exactly is the Eastside & what is the physical boundary?

OG eastsiders like Ulises Diaz and Luis Rodriguez tell me east of the Los Angeles River is the start of East LA. Others have said that it starts 2 miles west of the river, east of the 110 freeway. Many have called Silverlake, Echo Park & even East Hollywood part of the Eastside. Some people even say La Brea is the start of the Eastside. There has been talk of the Eastside indie rock circuit of Silverlake & Echo Park. The answer just depends on who it is, where they live and where they want to be down from.

Where is the Westside?

The Westside of Los Angeles really begins just west of La Cienega moving towards Robertson. Beverly Hills west is usually considered the start of the westside. West LA, Santa Monica, Brentwood, Westwood, Venice, Pacific Palisades & beyond.

Where is South Central?

There are many sheltered Angelenos that think South Central is anywhere south of the 10 Freeway. A 2007 exhibit at the California African-American Museum revealed the term "South Central" first appeared about 1920 in the vernacular language of the historic Black community living along Central Avenue. Especially the area around Central Avenue and Century Blvd. Watts is about 7 miles southeast of USC and the 10 Freeway. Nonetheless, the whole wide area south of the 10 has been lumped in as South Central, this giant pocket is well over 50 square miles. It's a huge part of southern Los Angeles comprised of small districts like Angeles Mesa, Canterbury Knolls, Jefferson Park, Green Meadows, Chesterfield Square, Manchester Square, Harvard Square and more. Over the last 40 years Leimert Park around Crenshaw and 43rd replaced Watts as the capital of the Black community.

Where is Orange County?

Ironically Orange County is statistically more urban than Los Angeles County. The explanation is that the whole northern third of LA County is desert & mountain land, while damn near every square foot of land in Orange County is packed with development. The OC is one of the most urban counties in America. Thanks to the TV showa "The OC," and "Laguna Beach," the OC calls itself as the "mecca" of cool. Some used to call it the "Orange Curtain."

Areas like Cerritos, Long Beach, Gardena and Carson are as diverse as any place in North America. It is here where you see the future of America. Among the generation growing up in this melting pot is a compassionate group of people concerned with keeping peace and building a better future. Some have called it utopian, our hopes lie in working together. Building community is where it's at. Pockets of community are villages in the sprawling mosaic. Bridge builders are wiring a circuitry of unity through the patchwork. For those willing to reach out of their comfort zone, the possibilities are endless and never boring.

Letters to My City

A poem of address, prose for what's next, generations of poets, generations of musicians, A city of artists, a freestyle fellowship, an academy of architects, designing nature based Solutions, the Garden City Movement, a sacred pilgrimage, bioregionalism, geographic Literacy, economy of experience, a monument to memory, memorize imagery before it's not here anymore

Sing one for the river, take out the technocrats, speak people first language, practice praxis, Put theory into practice, apply urban acupuncture, share a neighborhood story, an unwritten Elegy, the last day you ever saw your grandfather, your 4th grade teacher, movements of people, urban apostrophe, an arrival story, the landscape vernacular, behold the Central Library, the legacy of the Women's Building

One for Wanda, the spark of creation, on location, a city drive with your mother, a hug from your brother, a song about your sister, music is the heartbeat, a field of great streets, night and the city, the gospel of beauty, pound the pavement, fight the good fight, bridge the divide, grow something, put people over profit, celebrate the present, we are the movement

Acknowledgments

Thank you to Emi, Eka & Skye.
Pam Hays, Howard Sonksen, Amy Sonksen, Dr. Ron Hays, David Sonksen, Mary Elaine Sonksen, Frank Sibley, Terry Sibley.

Deep gratitude to Writ Large Press. Thank you Chiwan Choi for your vision & 20 years of friendship. Salute to Judeth Oden Choi & Peter Woods. Thank you for the countless hours we spent writing together F. Douglas Brown.

Gratitude to Rocio Carlos, Traci Kato-Kiriyama, Michael Tiger Foster, Tyler Reeb, Dr. Lauri Ramey, Mike Davis, Alessandra Moctezuma, Sesshu Foster, Luis J. Rodriguez, Rubén Guevara, Cal State L.A. & the CSULA English Department, Stella Adler Theater, Tim Wong, Lewis MacAdams, A.K. Toney, V. Zamora, Christian Lozada, Steve Isoardi, Tomas Benitez, Lucas Benitez, Jessica Ceballos y Campbell, Will McConnell, Doug Cremer, Douglas Kearney, Amy Uyematsu, Marisela Norte, Luivette Resto, Sara Borjas, Kim Koga, Elisabeth Sandberg, Steve Abee, Lynell George, Vickie Vertiz, Kenji Liu, Librecht Wanderlust, Ashaki M. Jackson, Pam Ward, Darren Cifarelli, Southwest College English Department, Cory Cofer, Dave Wittman, Jesse Bliss, Sunyoung Kim, Akiko Murakata, Mike Murase, Justin Cram, Yosuke Kitazawa, Juan Devis, Janice Lee, Adam Leipzig, Yasmin Dunn, Phillip Martin, Mear One, Black Bird, Jack Rodgers, David Lau, Terry Robinson, Armond Kinard, Miguel Gutierrez, Megan Jacobs, Miles Tackett, Carlos Guaico, Kamau Daaood, Shonda Buchanan, Allan Aquino, Dorothy Randall Gray, Jamie Fitzgerald Lahey, CheryL Klein, Joel Arquillos, 826LA, Obed Silva, East L.A. College English Department, David Romero, Elizabeth Moran, Tibbie Dunbar, Joe Gardner, Tanya Ko-Hong, Peter J. Harris, Alan Nakagawa, Steven Reigns, Teka Lark, Lee Boek, Lee Ballinger, Esotouric, Kim Cooper, Richard Schave, Victor Castelo, Phillip Medina, Jeremy Rosenberg, William A. Gonzalez,

Harold Terezon, Dante Mitchell, Monique Mitchell, Jamal Carter, Joseph Rios, Terrance Hayes, Terry Wolverton, Steph Cha, Naomi Hirahara, Trevon Kelley, Forrest Wilson, Juan Bueno, Tongo Eisen-Martin, Angel City Press, Paddy Calistro, Harriet Tubman Press, Lea Sibley Alvarez, Meris Sibley, Miguel Alvarez, Abraham Alvarez, Leo Imbert, Ko & Kate Maruyama, Natashia Deon, Def Sound, Poetry LA, Risa Williams, Peter Chesney and all of my students from the past, present and future. Thank you to everyone reading this.
Rest in Poetry: Frank Sibley Jr., Wanda Coleman, Carolyn See, Dr. Jim Garrett, Brian Sanchez, Jim Hodgkins, Lionel Rolfe, DJ Dusk & Arturo dela Torre

Thank you to the following books and anthologies for publishing some of these pieces originally:

Coiled Serpent,
Leimert Park Redux,
Los Angeles Union Station: Tracks to the Future,
Wide Awake: Poets from Los Angeles & Beyond.
Words Ignite: Explore, Write & Perform Classic & Spoken Word Poetry

Thank you to the following publications and websites for publishing some of these pieces, sometimes in an earlier version:

KCET, Poets & Writers, Entropy, Cultural Weekly, Lana Turner, Angel City Review, Angel's Flight, Eastside Rose, The Argonaut, The Architect's Newspaper, Brooklyn & Boyle, The 562, LA Taco.

ABOUT THE AUTHOR

Equally a scholar and performer, MIKE SONKSEN, also known as, MIKE THE POET, is a 3rd-generation L.A. native acclaimed for poetry performances, published articles and mentoring teen writers. Following his graduation from U.C.L.A. in 1997, he has published over 500 essays and poems with publications including the Academy of American Poets, *KCET*, *Poets & Writers Magazine*, *LA Weekly*, *OC Weekly*, *Lana Turner*, *Los Angeles Review of Books*, *Cultural Weekly*, *Entropy* and many others. Mike has an Interdisciplinary Master of Arts in English and History and his prose and poetry have been included in programs with the Mayor's Office, the Los Angeles Public Library's "Made in LA," series, Grand Park, the Music Center and the Friends of the Los Angeles River. Mike has taught at Cal State L.A., Southwest College and Woodbury University. In June of 2018 one of his *KCET* essays was awarded by the LA Press Club. Sonksen has also given Los Angeles city tours combining poetry and prose for the Metropolitan Transit Authority, City of Santa Monica, Museum of Architecture & Design, Museum of Neon Art, Craft & Folk Art Museum, Red Line Tours and California Excursions. Sonksen's poem "I Am Alive in Los Angeles!" was made into an art installation at 7th and Olive in Downtown Los Angeles.

OFFICIAL

THE ACCOMPLICES

GET OUT OF JAIL
∗ VOUCHER ∗

- -

Tear this out.

Skip that social event.

It's okay.

You don't have to go if you don't want to. Pick up
the book you just bought. Open to the first page.
You'll thank us by the third paragraph.

If friends ask why you were a no-show, show them
this voucher.
You'll be fine.

- -

We're thriving.